Acorn Guide to Northwest Wisconsin

Also by Tim Bewer

Wisconsin's Outdoor Treasures:
A Guide to 150 Natural Destinations

Acorn Guide to

Northwest Wisconsin
(Ashland, Bayfield, Burnett, Douglas, Sawyer, and Washburn counties)

Tim Bewer

PRAIRIE OAK PRESS
Madison, Wisconsin

First edition, first printing

Copyright ©1999 by Tim Bewer

All rights reserved. No part of this publication may be reproduced or transmitted in any form or by any means, electronic or mechanical, including photocopy, recording, or any information storage or retrieval system, without permission in writing from the publisher.

Prairie Oak Press
821 Prospect Place
Madison, Wisconsin 53703

Design by Prairie Oak Press
Typeset by Quick Quality Press, Madison, Wisconsin
Cover design by Flying Fish Graphics, Blue Mounds, Wisconsin
Cover photographs by Brent Nicastro
Printed in the United States of America by
BookCrafters, Chelsea, Michigan

Library of Congress Cataloging-In-Publication Data

Bewer, Tim, 1970–
Acorn guide northwest Wisconsin / Tim Bewer. -- 1st ed.
    p.   cm.
Includes index.
ISBN 1-879483-57-2 (alk. paper)
1. Wisconsin Guidebooks.   I. Title. II. Title: Northwest Wisconsin.
F579.3.B49   1999
917.7504'43--dc21   99-23993
                                                                                 CIP

CONTENTS

Introduction .... *vii*
1. Bayfield and the Apostle Islands **1**
    Bayfield 1
    The Greatest of the Great Lakes 4
    Madeline Island 13
    Getting to the Island 14
    Red Cliff Reservation 20
    Washburn 23
    Have County Seat, Will Travel 24

2. Endless Shores **31**
    Cornucopia 31
    Ho Ho Ho! 32
    Herbster 35
    Port Wing 37
    Aurora Borealis 39

3. Forest Primeval **40**
    Cable 40
    CAMBA 42
    Drummond 46
    Chequamegon National Forest 48
    Iron River 51

4. Garland City **55**
    Ashland 55
    Timeless Timber 60
    Bad River Reservation 65
    Mellen 67
    Glidden 70
    Elk 72

5. Twin Ports 74
Superior 74
Twin Ports Ship Watching 77
Tri-County Corridor 79
Duluth Attractions Guide 85
The Channel Battle 87
Port Town Trolley 93

6. Brule-St. Croix Highway 96
Solon Springs 96
North Country National Scenic Trail 98
Gordon 100
Brule 101

7. Lore of the Lumberjack 105
Hayward 105
Lac Courte Oreilles Reservation 118
The Ojibwe 120
Stone Lake 122

8. Land of 1,000 Lakes 126
Spooner 126
Snowmobiling 127
Shell Lake 130
Land O' Lakes 134
Trego 135
St. Croix National Scenic Riverway 136
Birchwood 138

9. St. Croix Valley 143
Grantsburg 143
Siren 147
Gandy Dancer Trail 147
Webster 150
Danbury 153
The St. Croix Ojibwe 154

Index 156

INTRODUCTION

Northwest Wisconsin is one of the Midwest's premier getaways. From incomparable Bayfield to family-friendly Hayward, the area has a long history of attracting vacationers. The entire region has a relaxed feeling. Beautiful old buildings, interesting museums, great restaurants, and classic B&Bs all bring people to the cities and small towns. National chains haven't made much of an advance into the area; you'll find mostly family-owned establishments where you will get real service with a friendly smile.

For nature lovers, this corner of the state has the broadest stretches of forests, the wildest rivers, and more lakes than you could ever visit in a lifetime, not to mention the wild shore and islands of Lake Superior. The world's largest lake offers some of the nation's best inland sailing and sea kayaking, particularly around the Apostle Islands, and there are plenty of opportunities for first-timers to try these exciting sports. The abundant parks and forests offer superb canoeing, hiking, and horseback riding. And, it's all closer than you think; by car, it's just one hour from Minneapolis/St. Paul, four hours from Madison, six hours from Milwaukee, and seven hours from Chicago.

I can remember visiting Superior as a child and being awed by the docks. When I was quite a bit older, Bayfield and the Apostle Islands had the same effect on me. And still nothing quite compares to walking along a deserted Lake Superior beach and hunting for agates while the waves gently crash on the shore. When I moved to the area I routinely discovered new and unique attractions that I now share with you. With this book you'll be able to discover your own little piece of paradise.

You'll find the obvious tourist destinations in this book, including an attractions guide for Duluth, Minnesota. This book covers these areas in more detail than any other guidebook, but I've also detailed many out-of-the-way places that you may never have heard of, such as Birchwood, Glidden, Grantsburg, and Stone Lake, that make good off-the-beaten-path destinations or short stops on the way to your main destination.

There is always something to see or do here, but September is my unchallenged pick for best time to visit the area: you'll find fall colors, cooler temperatures, fewer people, and few if any mosquitoes. The only downside is that some places close for the year after Labor Day, but the biggest and best sights and shops are open at least through the end of the month.

While Northwest Wisconsin is primarily a warm weather destination, the fun doesn't stop during the winter. There is downhill and cross-country skiing, dog sledding, ice caves, snow sculpture contests, sleigh rides, and casinos that draw gamblers year-round.

Bottom line—there is something for everyone in Northwest Wisconsin. I hope this book leads you to something memorable.

About This Book

Most chapters of this book cover one county. Bayfield and Douglas Counties are further divided. Out-of-the-way places such as state parks or remote resorts appear with the community that's closest by.

The information you need is always close at hand. Each community is divided into the following sections: Things to See and Do, Scenic Drive, Events, Shopping (focusing largely on antique stores and art galleries), Performing Arts, Golf, Marinas/Charters, Bicycling, Outdoor Rentals, Spectator Sports, Where to Eat, Where to Stay, Emergencies, and More Information.

A $ signifies an admission fee. Keep in mind that many places such as hotels or sailing charter companies offer early and late season discounts. But even during the summer high-season this area still offers vacationers a real bargain overall.

Your choice of lodging includes bed-and-breakfasts, fancy hotels, basic motels, resorts, developed campgrounds, remote island camping, and wilderness backpacking. Some of the smaller towns don't offer much choice, but you will always find something in nearby communities.

The **telephone area code** is 715 unless otherwise noted. The area codes 888 and 877 have joined 800 as toll-free area codes, and these are included whereever available.

Before You Go

For weekends between Memorial Day and Labor Day, it would be wise to make lodging reservations as far in advance as possible. This is not to say reservations are always necessary. For the most part you can find accommodations on short notice except on the weekends surrounding some of the biggest events—the American Birkebeiner, Bayfield Apple Festival, Lumberjack World Championships, or World

Championship Snowmobile Watercross. In some towns, tourism offices keep lists of vacancies and can book rooms for you.

The business hours that appear in the listings are as detailed as possible, but hours are subject to change, so call ahead if you are going out of your way to see something specific. Shopkeepers often open or close according to the number of vacationers. An early or late winter or spring often determines when an establishment opens or closes for the season. It's also not unusual to close up shop if it's a slow day, the weather is bad (or really good and they want to enjoy it too), they have a family gathering to attend, or they just feel like it. Keep in mind that if a place you had your heart set on seeing is closed, many museums and stores in the smaller towns will open up for you if you call ahead. Places listed here are open year-round, unless stated otherwise.

When you make reservations at a resort, be sure to ask what you need to bring; linens, dishes, and towels are not always provided or cost extra, and sometimes it depends on the unit you stay in or the season.

A Word About the Weather

Overall the summer climate is nearly perfect, though it can still get pretty hot some days. In fact, it was the climate, not the wonderful scenery, that prompted so many people from across the country to summer here around the turn of the century. The average temperature in July is 68 degrees. It rarely gets into the nineties. You can also count on the summer temperature being 5 to 10 degrees cooler near Lake Superior. The surrounding air is cooled by an average Lake Superior water temperature of just 40 degrees. This means you should always be cautious when boating, because if you fall into the lake hypothermia can set it quickly. It doesn't rule out swimming, however, since shallow bays frequently warm up to the sixties. Though winters are cold (the average January temperature is 9 degrees) plentiful snow is all but guaranteed, making the region perfect for winter sports enthusiasts.

Public Transport

Bay Area Rural Transit (BART) buses run between Red Cliff and Odanah connecting these towns with Ashland, Washburn, and Bayfield and will stop anywhere along the way. The buses operate Monday through Friday and are wheelchair accessible and have bike racks. Call 682-9664 for more information.

The **Duluth Transit Authority** bus system covers both Duluth and Superior and offers a fairly extensive service for a market this small (buses even go to Park Point [p. 88] and Spirit Mountain [p. 95]), though service is reduced after 7 p.m. and on weekends. During the warmer months DTA buses have bike racks available. Most buses are wheelchair accessible. Call 218/722-SAVE for schedules and information.

Greyhound operates between Duluth and Minneapolis/St. Paul several times a day. For reservations call 218/722-5591 or 800/231-2222.

From the Twin Cities you can ride **NWT Express** to Hayward or Spooner. The vans that run on Tuesdays, Thursdays, and Saturdays also stop in Rice Lake, Cumberland, and Turtle Lake. Prices are discounted for seniors and children and reservations are required. For more information call 634-5307, 800/262-8974.

Superior Transport goes once daily to Iron River and Ashland from the Greyhound Station in Duluth. Call 218/722-5591, 888/487-6511 for information.

Additional Information

Wisconsin Department of Tourism
201 W. Washington Ave.
P.O. Box 7976
Madison, WI 53707
608/266-2161
800/432-8747
www.tourism.state.wi.us

Wisconsin road conditions - 800/ROAD-WIS

Forest Service Fall Foliage Hotline - 800/354-4595

Chapter 1
Bayfield and the Apostle Islands
Bayfield, Madeline Island, Red Cliff Reservation, Washburn

Bayfield

Sure, people who found this scenic gem of a town on Lake Superior years ago like to hark back to the days before Bayfield was "discovered," but it still doesn't get much better than this. Despite the influx of tourists each summer, one of Bayfield's main attractions is the tranquillity: you can't help but escape the daily grind here. You won't find any traffic lights, parking meters, or fast food chains in this city of just 678 permanent residents. What you will find is a scenic view around every corner, art galleries for every taste, a plethora of indulgent bed-and-breakfasts, fine dining, scrumptious treats, fascinating attractions, and so many exquisite turn-of-the-century buildings perched on the hills overlooking the lake that most of the town has been designated a National Historic District. If this wasn't enough, it is surrounded by some of the most beautiful wilderness anywhere. We can only hope it won't be ruined by Bayfield's increasing popularity.

The town was named for Admiral Henry Bayfield of the British Royal Navy, who charted Chequamegon Bay between 1823 and 1825 and determined that a deep-water harbor could be developed here. No development could take place, however, until after 1854 when the Ojibwe signed a treaty ceding most of their land. Just two years later Henry Rice, a member of the Minnesota territorial legislature, started the Bayfield Land Company here, anticipating a rail connection with St. Paul. Settlers and investors soon arrived with dreams of a shipping center to rival Chicago.

Though it was many years before the iron rails reached Bayfield, the town still prospered, as evidenced by the many elaborate Queen Anne and Italianate homes built here. Brownstone was quarried on several islands and the mainland, sawmills sprang up to facilitate logging, and by the end of the century wealthy families had discovered it as a summer escape.

The most successful industry was commercial fishing, which thrived through the first half of the century. At their peak in the 1940s Bayfield's fisheries annually shipped as many as 25 million pounds of lake trout, whitefish, and lake herring. By the 1950s overfishing and the invasion of sea lamprey devastated the industry. Commercial fishing has survived, but despite lamprey control and new fishing laws it pales in comparison to those bountiful earlier decades. Tourism, which has rebounded, is now the keystone of the economy.

Things to See and Do

The **Apostle Islands National Lakeshore Visitor Center** with historical displays and a short film that can be viewed upon request offers an overview of the area, making this a good first stop in town. You shouldn't miss the large Fresnel lens from the Michigan Island lighthouse if you've never seen one before. A good selection of books and maps is on sale here too. The center is in the restored Bayfield County Courthouse, a beautiful brownstone built in 1883 and listed on the National Register of Historic Places. After the county seat moved to Washburn (see p. 24) in 1892 the building served as a school and as a World War II German prisoner-of-war camp, among other things. Located at 415 Washington Ave., 779-3397. Open 8–4:30 daily, May 1 through Memorial Day weekend; then 8–6 daily through Labor Day, 8–5 through mid-October; and 8–4:30 the rest of the year. Wheelchair accessible.

The **Apostle Islands National Lakeshore**, 21 islands (all of the Apostles but Madeline) and 12 miles of shore on the mainland, with its famous sea caves and shoreline cliffs, offers incomparable beauty. It was first proposed as a national park in 1891, when wealthy eastern families summered here. The National Park Service considered but rejected the idea in 1930, by which time logging had largely devastated the islands (though some old-growth forest remains). Slowly the land recovered and the park was established in 1970. What you choose to do here is limited only by your imagination. Sailors and kayakers consider this some of the nation's prime inland aquatic terrain. Hiking trails cross half of the islands, with Stockton and Oak offering the most miles. The caves, cliffs, shipwrecks, and high visibility make this a popular place to scuba dive. The park service offers summer nature and historical programs. There are 64 campsites on half the islands (call 779-3397 for reservations, **$**), and backpacking (with free permit) is allowed in most places. Winter visitors, who arrive in greater numbers each year, can ski, snowshoe, dogsled, explore ice caves, or camp.

Besides the islands' natural scenery, there are some fascinating historic sites, all listed on the National Register of Historic Places. Five of the islands' six **lighthouses** (all but the La Pointe Lighthouse on Long Island) are open to visitors daily from late June through early September. The Raspberry Island Lighthouse, open for guided tours daily from early June through September, re-creates the keeper's home life. Now automated and equipped with radio beacons, the lighthouses are still used for navigation. The **Manitou Island Fish Camp** reflects the harsh life of winter fishing. It is open early June through early September.

The **visitor centers** at Little Sand Bay (p. 21) and on Stockton Island have interesting exhibits. See page 33 for more National Lakeshore information.

The easiest way to see the islands if you don't have your own boat is with **Apostle Islands Cruise Service**. It offers a wide variety of tour options, the most popular being the three-hour narrated Grand Tour which passes most of the islands, including the Devils Island sea caves and several lighthouses, but makes no stops. Other tours feature lighthouses and sea caves and some make stops on Manitou, Oak, Sand, Stockton, and Raspberry Islands. The water taxi can take up to six people to any of the islands. Another option is to sail aboard the 54-foot, three-masted wooden schooner **Zeeto**. Private charters are available. Boats depart from City Dock at the end of Rittenhouse Avenue, 779-3925, 800/323-7619. Tours run daily, mid-May to mid-October, though not all trips are available all the time; call for schedules or information. Some trips are wheelchair accessible. **$**

While Apostle Islands Cruise Service makes seeing the islands as easy as possible, **Trek and Trail** allows you to really explore the area. It offers over a dozen sea kayaking trips and instructional courses ranging from relaxed half-day paddles to week-long circumnavigations of the islands. It also arranges kayaking trips in other locations, from North Carolina to Scotland. In the winter you can experience dogsledding on the mainland or head out to the islands on the frozen lake. Located at 222 Rittenhouse Ave., 779-3595, 800/354-8735. **$**

The **Bayfield Heritage Association Museum** has a variety of exhibits from the town's early history including a barbershop, telephone switchboard, and many old photos. Located at 30 N. Broad St., 779-5958. Open 1–4 Wednesday–Sunday from Memorial Day weekend to Labor Day.

In the **Booth Cooperage Museum**, built in 1900 and now listed on the National Register of Historic Places, as many as 15,000 barrels a year were made for shipping the catch of the Booth fisheries. Located on Washington Avenue across from the ferry landing. Call 747-2051 for more information.

The **Bayfield State Fish Hatchery**, the third opened in Wisconsin and now listed on the National Register of Historic Places, produces more than a million fish annually, over 90 percent of which are destined for Lake Superior. In the exhibit area are educational displays, a tank with native fish, and indoor fish-raising tanks. Outside you can see fish in the ponds behind the buildings, and during the spring and fall you can watch spawning fish on Pike's Creek behind the facility. Located 2.5 miles south on Hwy 13, 779-5430. Open 8–3:30 weekdays and 8–3 weekends. Wheelchair accessible.

The Greatest of the Great Lakes

To call Lake Superior big is a colossal understatement. Just take a look at the numbers. It covers 31,280 square miles, the largest surface area of any lake in the world and equal to Massachusetts, Connecticut, Rhode Island, Vermont, and New Hampshire. It stretches 350 miles at its longest part, 160 miles at its widest; it has 2,730 miles of shoreline; and its deepest point is 1,402 feet below the surface. It holds three quadrillion (that's 15 zeros) gallons of water: this constitutes one-eighth of the world's supply of fresh water, enough to cover all of North and South America one foot deep. Only Lake Baikal in Siberia, a much deeper lake, contains more. It isn't just the volume of water that makes this lake special; it happens to be some of the purest and cleanest water in the world.

Though the lake is usually enchanting it also has a dark side. During the worst storms, waves can rage over 30 feet tall. At least 350 ships have wound up on the bottom of the lake, including the famous *Edmund Fitzgerald*, which was snapped in half near Sault Ste. Marie, Michigan, sending all 29 crew members aboard the 729-foot ore carrier to a watery grave on November 10, 1975. It's easy to see why those who are intimately familiar with the lake will tell you that Superior qualifies as an inland sea.

In addition to the historic structures already mentioned, the ones that follow are also worth a quick look. If you would like more information, the booklet **Brownstone and Bargeboard: A Walking Tour of Historic Bayfield** is for sale in many shops.

Christ Church, the first Episcopal church in northern Wisconsin, looks like a giant gingerbread house. The 1870 building at 125 N. Third St. is listed on the National Register of Historic Places.

The **Bayfield Public Library**, a brownstone and brick building built in 1903 by Andrew Carnegie, is located at the corner of N. Broad Street and Washington Avenue.

Half a block east of the library on Washington Avenue is the city's old **jail**. The small square fieldstone building with iron grating over the windows and doors was built in 1926.

The 230-foot **Iron Bridge** with its beautiful arched trusses was built in 1912. It replaced a wood bridge that collapsed just after a herd of cows passed over it. Now a pedestrian walkway, the bridge is along Rice Avenue between Second and Third Streets, but is best viewed from below near the intersection of Washington Avenue and N. Broad Street.

The **Iron Bridge Nature Trail**, one of two hiking trails in Bayfield, starts below the Iron Bridge and follows a narrow creek up the deep, wooded ravine for about a quarter mile. You'll find benches for a quiet rest, historical markers along the trail, and small waterfalls near the top.

The other trail, the **RR Hiking Trail**, follows the beautiful lakeshore on an abandoned railroad grade for three miles south to Port Superior Marina. The unmarked path begins at the corner of Third Street and Manypenny Avenue.

Mt. Ashwabay (ASHland-WAshburn-BAYfield) with 13 downhill runs for skiers and snowboarders and 40 km of cross-country ski trails is the main winter attraction here. Rentals and instruction are available. Located 4 miles south on Hwy 13, then 1.5 miles west on Ski Hill Road, 779-3227. **$**

The **Apostle Highlands Ski Trails**, at the Apostle Highlands Golf Course (p. 9), have 5.6 km of groomed cross-country trails with spectacular views of Chequamegon Bay. There is a "chalet" with a ski shop and snacks. Open 9–4 Thursday–Sunday. **$**

Though the swimming season is short there are two beaches in town: **Washington Avenue Beach** is located next to the ferry landing at the end of its namesake road; **Broad Street Beach** (also known as Reiten Beach) is at the end of—surprise!—S. Broad Street. The latter is cleared for ice skating in the winter. A warming shelter and free use of skates are available 5–9 Wednesday and 1–6 Saturday and Sunday.

Kids will also enjoy **East End Park**, which has a playground, picnic area, volleyball court, and wheelchair-accessible fishing pier. Located next to the marina at the end of S. First Street.

Events

The **Bayfield Apple Festival**, held the first weekend in October, is such a huge affair that the town can barely hold the 50,000 or so people who attend each year. The long-time celebration of this beloved fruit features a plethora of apple foods, from the obvious pies, cider, and caramel apples to the obscure—ever tried apple bratwurst, apple mustard, or apple ice cream? The most hotly contested event is the apple peeling competition; the current record is 291.75 inches. Another competition not to be missed is the night parade of brightly and creatively lit boats. Throughout the event you can enjoy live music on several stages, street performers, an arts and crafts fair, orchard tours, hay rides, carnival rides, and a parade. The biggest event of the weekend is the mass band when over 500 marching musicians play "On, Wisconsin."

Shopping

This may be a small town, but you can shop 'til you drop. Early in the century merchants were accused of letting cows roam the streets to make people step into their stores. Today you can hardly get some people out.

None of the antique stores in Bayfield is very large, but the selection is high quality. They include **Antiques at Twenty North First**, 20 N. First St., 779-3909, open daily, May through October; **Blue Water Antiques**, 104 Rittenhouse Ave., 779-2381, open daily, May through October, and irregular hours the rest of the year; **Harbor Gifts & Antiques**, 33 N. Front St., 779-3962, open daily. **Sally's**, an eclectic open-air shop, is a whole other story. There are some real gems piled along both sides of the highway here, but you'll have to sort through a lot of stuff to find them. Located half a mile north on Hwy 13. No set hours, but generally open daily, May through October.

You can buy fresh and smoked fish direct from the source at **Bay Fisheries**, 779-3910, open daily, May through October, and **Bodin Fisheries**, 779-3301, open Monday–Saturday. Both are located on the south side of town at the commercial fishing docks along Wilson Avenue.

The **Bayfield Artists Guild** is run by the 14 regional artists (some of whom work on their art while working the register) whose work is sold here. Browse through pottery, painting, jewelry, forged ironwork, wood carving, clothing, and even harp music. Located at 104 Rittenhouse Ave., 779-5781. Open daily, May through October.

Chapman House Gallery has creative blown and stained glass work plus some glass jewelry and a few paintings. Located at the corner of First Street and Rittenhouse Avenue, 779-9576, 888/422-9343. Open May to early October.

Eckels Pottery is run by the father and daughter team of Bob and Dede Eckels. Eckels has been around since 1960 and features handcrafted stoneware and porcelain from several resident artists. Besides the basics you'll find some very creative work. There's almost always someone in the shop working and you're welcome to watch. Located just south of town on Hwy 13, 779-5617. Open daily.

First Street Gallery features a bit little of everything by many area artists. Browse through paintings, pottery, jewelry, stained glass, and clothing. Located at 100 Rittenhouse Ave., 779-5101. Open May to mid-October.

Everything for sale at **Keeper of the Light** has a lighthouse or nautical theme from basic souvenirs to fine art. Located at 19 N. Front St., 779-5619, 800/779-4487. Open daily.

At **Kerr Studio & Gallery** you'll find the metallic sculpture of Brian Kerr. There is also jewelry, and don't miss the outdoor sculpture. Located at 21 N. Front St., 779-5790, 888/358-6029. Open daily, May to mid-October, and irregular hours the rest of the year, but it is usually open.

L'Atelier is one of Bayfield's oldest, and favorite, boutiques. Many of the clothes, kitchen accessories, and assorted other items have an ethnic flare. Located at 13 S. Second St., 779-5159. Open May through October.

Sivertson Gallery is well known for its "art of the north." The paintings, limited edition prints, photography, and sculpture here are created by regional and Native American artists. Located at 117 Rittenhouse Ave., 779-9616, 888/329-5282. Open daily, May through mid-October, and then weekends through December.

Pottery, made in the on-site studio, is just one of the items for sale at **Stone's Throw**, Bayfield's most enjoyable gallery to browse. Painting, photography, woodwork, basketry, jewelry, and other items made by local artists, as well as stationery, hats, and other small gift items, are all available here too. Also on display are the remains of a 1919 fishing boat and Johnny Appleseed, a puppet that stands over 20 feet tall and marches each year in the Apple Festival parade. Located at 40 S. Second St., 779-5200. Open daily, May through mid-October, and weekends through December; the gallery might be open other times if potters are working in the studio.

Thanks to Lake Superior's moderating effect on the climate, 18 **orchards and berry farms** dot the hills around Bayfield. Follow Hwy J, which loops around town, and let your taste buds guide you. The bounty changes with the season, but you can expect to find apples, strawberries, cherries, raspberries, blueberries, pears, and plums between spring and fall. No matter when you're here you'll find something delectable since a wide variety of items, such as apple cider, jams and jellies, maple syrup, honey, flowers, pickles, and cheese, is available in any season. Some places also supplement the food inventory with crafts, antiques, and other items, which can make this a very productive shopping excursion. Most are open daily, May through October, and some continue on weekends through the rest of the year.

Performing Arts

Ballyhoo! **Big Top Chautauqua** hosts Warren Nelson and crew's original "house show" musicals celebrating the people and places of the Lake Superior region. National and regional musicians and many other events play here too, under a 750-capacity canvas tent, the most unique venue in the Northwoods. Some of the musicians who have performed at the "Carnegie Hall of tent shows" include Arlo Guthrie, Judy Collins, Leo Kottke, Bruce Cockburn, Bela Fleck, Garrison Keillor, and the Kingston Trio. You can easily take the big top home with you: CDs, cassettes, and videos are for sale, and Tent Show Radio is heard nationwide on public radio stations. Located at Mt. Ashwabay, four miles south on Hwy 13 then 1.5 miles west on Ski Hill Road, 373-5552, 888/BIG-TENT. A free shuttle runs daily from Red Cliff and Saturdays from Ashland, picking up passengers at several points along the way. The season runs from early June into September, and shows are held almost nightly. Wheelchair accessible. $

The public is invited to free **chamber music concerts** at historic Christ Church on Thursday nights at 5 between July and mid-August, during the Apple Festival (p. 6), and during the Blessing of the Fleet in June. Sherry and hors d'oeuvres are served after the performances. Located at 125 N. Third St., 779-3401.

Golf

The challenging 18-hole **Apostle Highlands Golf Course**, one mile west on Manypenny Avenue, 779-5960, is perched 500 feet above Lake Superior.

Marinas/Charters

Apostle Islands Marina, downtown at the end of S. First Street, 779-5661, is a full service marina with 140 slips for transient and seasonal dockage.

Port Superior Marina, two miles south on Hwy 13, 779-5360, is a full service marina with 200 slips for transient and seasonal dockage.

The following companies offer sailing trips: **Animaashi Sailing Co.**, 779-5468, 888/272-4548; **Catchun-Sun Charters**, 779-3111, 888/724-5494; **Moon Shadow Sailing**, 612/757-6498; **Sailboats Inc.**, 779-3269, 800/826-7010, also has bareboat charters and instruction available; **Superior Charters**, 779-5124, 800/772-5124, also has bareboat charters and instruction available. Options offered by most companies include half day, full day, sunset, overnight, and multi-day trips.

If you want to do more than just sight-see on Lake Superior **Nourse's Sport Fishing**, 779-3253, 800/779-3257, and **Roberta's Charters**, 779-5744, offer fishing charters.

Bicycling

Bikes are allowed on the **RR Hiking Trail** (p. 5).

Outdoor Rentals

Apostle Islands Cruise Service, located at City Dock at the end of Rittenhouse Avenue, 779-9575, 800/323-7619, rents kayaks.

Apostle Islands Outfitters & General Store, 10 S. Broad St., 779-3411, rents snowshoes. This is also the place to pick up any camping supplies you left at home.

Trek and Trail, 222 Rittenhouse Ave., 779-3595, 800/354-8735, rents kayaks, bikes, and offers a shuttle service.

Spectator Sports

You can watch **car races** on Lake Superior on weekend afternoons during January and February.

Where to Eat

The **Egg Toss Cafe**, 41 Manypenny Ave., 779-5181, serves only breakfast but stays open through the lunch hour. You'll find omelets, huevos rancheros, quiche, steak and eggs, French toast, pancakes, fresh bakery, and everything else you'd hope to find on a breakfast menu. It has a screened porch. Open daily.

Greunke's First Street Inn, 17 Rittenhouse Ave., 779-5480, 800/245-3072, has a beloved 1950s decor, including a classic 1946 Wurlitzer jukebox and enough Coca-Cola memorabilia to start a museum. Seafood (including whitefish livers) is the specialty, but the menu also features steak, barbecued ribs, chicken, sandwiches, pasta, and prime rib on Fridays and Saturdays. Greunke's also has nightly outdoor fish boils, Memorial Day weekend to Labor Day. Or you can just sit at the bar and get a malted or burger. Open daily for breakfast, lunch, and dinner, April through October.

The **Harbor Lights Dining Room** at the Bayfield Inn, 20 Rittenhouse Ave., 779-3363, where both the dining room and the rooftop garden overlook the lake and marina, has the best views of any restaurant in town. The slightly upscale menu specializes in seafood but also features steak and pasta. You'll find various ethnic specials on Thursdays plus the usual Friday fish fry and Saturday prime rib. Open for lunch and dinner daily, Memorial Day weekend through early October, and Wednesday–Sunday the rest of the year.

Maggie's, 257 Manypenny Ave., 779-5641, is a perennial favorite of locals and tourists alike. It's as famous for its food as it is for the flamingos, which are on everything but the menu. The creative menu does have sandwiches, fajitas, salads, pizza, whitefish livers, and daily specials. Recommended entrees include the bison burger, spicy black bean nachos, and penne with wild mushrooms and smoked duck. The bar has numerous microbrews, imported beers, and a good wine list. During nice weather you can enjoy drinks on the outdoor deck. Open daily for lunch and dinner.

Minnie's Coffee & Tea House, 117 Rittenhouse Ave., 779-9619, uses organic and/or locally grown ingredients in most of its food and drinks, which is one reason it all tastes so good. Besides the obvious beverages there are also fresh bakery and soups. Open daily for breakfast, lunch, and dinner, May through October, and reduced hours the rest of the year.

The **Old Rittenhouse Inn**, 301 Rittenhouse Ave., 779-5111, is Bayfield's most elegant dining experience in Bayfield's most beloved home, an imposing 1880 Queen Anne–style Victorian mansion. The creative, unwritten menu of regional specialties changes daily, but you won't be disappointed. Fresh, local ingredients are used whenever possible. Event dinners, such as wassail dinner concerts, occur frequently throughout the year. A cookbook is for sale so you can take some of their wonderful recipes home with you. Dinner daily, May through October, and weekends the rest of the year; lunch daily, June through September; call about breakfast. Reservations required.

Though not exactly cheap, the **Pier Plaza**, across from the city dock at the Bay Front Inn, 779-3330, has some of the best prices in Bayfield. And since the food is good this place is frequently packed. The menu includes seafood, sandwiches, pizza, homemade soups, salad bar, fresh bakery and pies, plus daily specials including a Friday fish fry and barbecued hickory ribs on Saturday. There are great views of the lake and marina from the dining room and the outdoor patio. Open daily in summer for breakfast, lunch, and dinner; usually closed for a few months during the winter.

Where to Stay

It can be difficult to find a room on short notice during summer months or even well in advance during peak weekends. The Chamber of Commerce, 800/447-4094, which keeps a list of vacancies, can help.

Bed-and-Breakfasts

The **Apple Tree Inn**, half a mile south on Hwy 13, 779-5572, 800/400-6532 (pin 2916), an authentically restored early-1900s farmhouse with a relaxing front porch, sits on a three-acre yard with several gardens. There are four guest rooms with private attached baths. A full breakfast is served in the sunroom, which has a fireplace and overlooks Lake Superior.

Baywood Place, 20 N. Third St., 779-3690, 800/993-3690, is a charming 1930 prairie-style bungalow with a sun porch and a quiet yard. The four guest rooms have private attached baths. A full gourmet breakfast is served in the dining room.

Cooper Hill House, 33 S. Sixth St., 779-5060, is in a classic 1888 home. The four antique-filled guest rooms have private baths. After a day of exploring Bayfield you can relax on the porch overlooking the lake or in front of the fireplace. A continental breakfast is served in the dining room.

The acclaimed **Old Rittenhouse Inn**, 301 Rittenhouse Ave., 779-5111, is the last word in luxury. There are 20 antique-filled guest rooms in three beautiful Victorian homes plus a private cottage. All have private attached baths and fireplaces, and many have whirlpools. Even the lowest priced rooms are fancy, but if you can afford it, you will be truly pampered. The Inn hosts many special events, such as mystery weekends and wine weekends. Guests are served a continental breakfast. Children are welcome.

The **Pinehurst Inn at Pike's Creek**, 3.75 miles south on Hwy 13, 779-3676, is a grand mansion built in 1885 by lumber baron R. D. Pike. The first thing you notice are the sandstone pillars and front wall, but the elaborate woodwork inside is just as impressive. It has six guest rooms with private baths, all but one attached, including a three-room whirlpool suite on the third floor. Guests are served a full breakfast in the formal dining room.

Other Lodging

Apostle Islands Rentals, 117 S. First St., 779-3621, 800/842-1199, rents condominiums in four different Bayfield locations. Options range from studios to four bedrooms and from simple to luxurious.

Bay Front Inn, 15 N. Front St., 779-3880, 888/243-4191, has 16 rooms on the lakefront with cable TV and a free continental breakfast. Some of the rooms have Jacuzzis, fireplaces, and private decks with lake views.

The Bayfield Inn, 20 Rittenhouse Ave., 779-3363, has 21 rooms on the lake at City Dock with cable TV, sauna, and free continental breakfast.

The city-owned **Dalrymple Park**, 0.5 mile north on Hwy 13, has 30 wooded campsites (15 electric) on Lake Superior. Open mid-May to mid-October.

Greunke's First Street Inn, 17 Rittenhouse Ave., 779-5480, 800/245-3072, may not be the absolute fanciest place in Bayfield, but it was good enough for John Kennedy Jr. This Bayfield institution has served as a lodging house since 1866, but don't worry, they've updated it since then. There are 12 rooms, many with period furnishings, in two historic houses, built in 1863 and 1880. Some rooms have cable TV and a few share baths.

Harbor's Edge Motel, 33 N. Front St., 779-3962, has 20 rooms, including some kitchenettes and a two-bedroom suite, with cable TV. Half the rooms are in a historic home while the others are in a newer building; both buildings overlook the lake and a small flower garden.

Isaac Wing House, 17 S. First St., 779-3907, 888/320-5468, has four suites with cable TV. Two of the suites have two bedrooms and all but one have a Jacuzzi. The classic 1854 home overlooks the marina.

Seagull Bay Motel, Hwy 13 at S. Seventh St., 779-5558, has 24 rooms, including some kitchenettes, and a three-bedroom cottage also with a kitchen. All units overlook the lake and have cable TV. There is direct access to the RR Hiking Trail (p. 5).

Silvernail Guest House, 249-1/2 Rittenhouse Ave., 779-5575, has four whirlpool suites, one with two bedrooms, and free continental breakfast in a beautifully restored 1887 New England saltbox.

Winfield Inn, at the north end of town on Hwy 13, 779-3252, has 31 rooms, including some two-bedroom units and kitchenettes, with cable TV. The beautiful deck and gardens, like all the rooms, overlook the lake.

Also see the **Apostle Islands National Lakeshore** (p. 2) for camping.

Emergencies

Call 373-6120. The nearest hospital is in Ashland.

More Information

Bayfield Chamber of Commerce, P.O. Box 138, Bayfield 54814, 779-3335, 800/447-4094, www.bayfield.org. The chamber offices are located at Manypenny Avenue and S. Broad Street.

Madeline Island

Madeline, the largest of the Apostle Islands (14 miles long by 3 miles wide) and the only one with commercial development, is just a 20-minute ferry ride from Bayfield. It isn't exactly remote and isolated anymore, but if you get beyond La Pointe, the island's only town, it still feels that way. And you will notice that island life is just a little more laid back, especially in the evening when the day-trippers have returned to the mainland.

The one-room school remains a part of island life here with children experiencing this bit of yesteryear through the fifth grade before they take the ferry to Bayfield for school. The pace of life does pick up noticeably in the summer when the 180 or so hardy souls who reside on "the Island" year-round are joined by 2,500 or so part-time residents.

The Ojibwe preceded the island's first European residents, and it remains their spiritual home. A 200-acre portion of the Bad River

Reservation sits at the far eastern end of the island. At its peak the Ojibwe population reached as high as 15,000 people, and during the lean winter months the island's medicine men practiced cannibalism until villagers rose up in defiance and executed them. The island was then abandoned for many years out of fear of the spirits of the medicine men's victims.

Beginning in the late seventeenth century, when France established the first trading post here, this became one of the most important fur trade centers for the entire Lake Superior and Upper Mississippi Region. Commercial fishing was another important island industry.

In 1793 Michel Cadotte, sent by the North West Company, arrived on the island and later married *Equaysayway* (Traveling Woman), daughter of Chief White Crane. To honor the union the chief changed the island's original Ojibwe name, *Moningwana Neiasha* (Isle of the Golden-Breasted Woodpecker), to Madeline, Equaysayway's baptismal name.

Getting to the Island

Unless you have your own boat you'll need to hop aboard the Madeline Island Ferry in Bayfield for the 2.6-mile ride to La Pointe. You can save a good chunk of money by leaving your car in Bayfield and just walking on. The ferry runs from breakup to freezeup, which is usually March through mid-January. For more information call 747-2051 or check www.madferry.com.

In the winter you can drive there on the ice road, officially Hwy H, which is marked by old Christmas trees. A passenger-only windsled (a propeller-driven boat) makes the trip while the ice is thin. If the lake doesn't freeze—which is rare—the ferry runs year-round.

Things to See and Do

The **Madeline Island Historical Museum**, operated by the State Historical Society of Wisconsin, has historical displays ranging from Ojibwe culture to Great Lakes commercial fishing. The main building, which houses most of the displays, is a combination of four nineteenth-century log buildings: an American Fur Company warehouse, the old jail, a pioneer barn, and an old cabin. The newer building has additional displays plus film and slide programs and a gift shop. Many special events are held here too. Located at 226 Colonel Woods Ave., 747-2415. Open 10–4 daily, late May to mid-October; 10–6, early July to late August. Wheelchair accessible. **$**

Relive the days of the one-room schoolhouse at **Lake View School**. The fully furnished 1905 school was moved here from the north end of the island and restored by the Madeline Island Historic Preservation Association. Located at 273 Colonel Woods Ave. It is open whenever volunteers are available from June through August, but if it's closed you can get a good look through the windows. Wheelchair accessible.

Get more information on these and seven other historic buildings by picking up the "**Downtown La Pointe Historic Walking Tour**" brochure at the chamber offices.

The **La Pointe Indian Cemetery**, established in 1836, is a burial site for both Native Americans and Europeans. Those buried here include Michel Cadotte and Chief Buffalo, Ojibwe chief when the La Pointe Treaty of 1854 was signed. The small houses covering some of the graves were adopted by Christianized Ojibwe to protect the dead and the food left with them. It is listed on the National Register of Historic Places. Located next to the marina, on Old Fort Road, one mile south of the ferry dock.

Just south of the cemetery is **Ojibway Memorial Park**. Here, in a small stand of pine trees next to a pond, is the grave of O-Shaka, son of Chief Buffalo. Both are sacred spots to the Ojibwe.

Joni's Beach on Lake Superior is a good place to cool off. There is also a picnic area, playground, and boat launch. Located three blocks south of the ferry dock on Main Street.

If your kids (or you) have a hankering for some putt-putt, **Madeline Mini-Golf** has got it covered. It also has video games. Located across from the museum, 747-3000. Open 10–10, Memorial Day weekend to Labor Day, then 11–7 through early October. **$**

Tom's Burned Down Cafe & Phoenix Gallery, which grew out of the ashes of Leona's Restaurant, is much more than just a bar with a Caribbean atmosphere; this is the island's primary work of folk art. The open air bar combines a canvas top, semi-truck trailer, palm fronds, sculptures, and hand-painted signs imparting wisdom. One of those signs, "Like Chaos Unraveling," describes it best, but once you're done taking it all in, you can't help but relax. Live music on weekends plus art demos and exhibitions round out the experience. Located at 1 Middle Rd., 747-6100. Open 11–late, mid-May to mid-October, weather permitting.

The **Capser and Nucy Meech hiking trails**, maintained by the Madeline Island Wilderness Preserve, wind for about two miles through a beautiful forest east of town. You can pick up a map or ask about scheduled nature walks at the chamber offices. The main trailhead is half a mile northeast of town on Big Bay Road.

Big Bay State Park covers 2,418 acres at the southeast corner of the island. The park's shoreline features a long beach and jagged cliffs which are especially fascinating in the winter. Inland is the beautiful 200-acre Big Bay Lagoon surrounded by thick forests and rolling hills. Six miles of hiking trails cross the park, and the shallow bay is a great place to swim. There are also seasonal nature programs, picnic areas, and a campground with 60 sites (wheelchair-accessible site), showers, and a dump station. Located five miles east of La Pointe (take Hwy H to Hagen Road), 747-6425, 779-4020 (off-season). Open year-round. $

On the other side of the bay is **Big Bay Town Park**, which has a footbridge leading to the beach and a campground with 40 sites (five electric, wheelchair-accessible sites). Paddlers can access Big Bay Lagoon from here: call **Bog Lake Outfitters**, 747-2685, to rent a canoe, rowboat, or paddle boat at the park.

Madeline Island Bus Tours are the easiest way to see the island. Join a local guide for a two-hour morning or afternoon tour of the island that includes a half-hour stop at Big Bay State Park. Tours leave from 825 Main St., 747-2051, and run late June to early September. $

For a unique winter experience join **Madeline Island Dog Sled Trips** on a day trip or winter camping adventure on Madeline Island or across the lake to other islands. Tents, sleeping bags, and meals provided. Trips leave from the Island Inn. Call 747-2000 for more information. $

Events

The **Chequamegon Chefs Exhibition**, held in June, is a chance to sample creative cuisine from the region's top chefs. $

Shopping

Dockside Gifts, a long-time island shop, is often packed with browsers waiting for the next ferry. It sells a variety of nautical, nature, and island-related gifts and souvenirs. Located at the ferry dock, 747-5492. Open daily, May through at least October, may stay open as late as December.

Waterfront Gallery features pottery, paintings, prints, and custom framing plus lots of unique craft and gift items and yard decorations. Don't miss the back rooms. Located one block north of the ferry dock on Main Street, 747-6996. Open daily, mid-May to early October.

The **Woods Hall Craft Shop** is a cooperative displaying the works of dozens of island artisans. It is best known for the hand-woven rugs made with on-site looms (you'll almost always find people working on them) but also sells pottery, jewelry, clothing, and more. They can do also do custom weaving from your design. Located three blocks south of the ferry dock, 747-3943. Open daily, Memorial Day weekend to early October.

Performing Arts

The **Madeline Island Music Camp** holds weekend concerts by gifted young musicians and camp faculty at the Clubhouse Restaurant and other locations from mid-June to mid-July. Call 747-2561 for information. $

Golf

The **Madeline Island Golf Club**, one mile south of the ferry dock, 747-3212, is one of the state's top courses. The challenging 18-hole Scottish links–style course was designed by the renown Robert Trent Jones Sr.

Marinas/Charters

The **Madeline Island Yacht Club**, one mile south of the ferry dock, 747-2655, offers seasonal and transient dockage at its 120-slip full service marina.

For bareboat or captained sailing charters call the **Apostle Islands Yacht Charter Association**, 800/821-3480, based at the Madeline Island Yacht Club. They also offer sailing classes.

Bicycling

With good paved roads and few hills, the island is a great place to bike.

Outdoor Rentals

Bike rentals are available all over town. **Motion To Go**, 102 Middle Rd., 747-6585, also has mopeds for rent.

Where to Eat

The Clubhouse, one mile south of the ferry dock, 747-2612, is one of the state's top restaurants. The constantly evolving menu features many natural local ingredients. Home-smoked Lake Superior trout and whitefish with local baby greens and walnut parmesan vinaigrette; or honey-glazed duck breast with wild rice risotto cake, scallion carrot salad, and spicy Asian barbecue sauce are examples of some of the exquisite meals you might enjoy. Other dishes feature lamb, venison, or lobster. The meals are complemented by the award-winning international wine list with over 300 vintages to choose from. The 12-sided glass building has plenty of good views to go around. Open for dinner only; weekends only in May and October, Friday–Sunday in June, Wednesday–Sunday in July and August, Thursday–Sunday in September. Reservations required. Free shuttle from the ferry dock.

Grampa Tony's, half a block south of the ferry dock on Main Street, 747-3911, a long-time island establishment, serves pizza, sandwiches (the garlic burger is a favorite), salads, and ice cream and has an espresso bar in a casual setting with indoor and outdoor seating. Open daily for breakfast and lunch plus dinner on Friday and Saturday from early May through Memorial Day weekend and then daily for breakfast, lunch, and dinner through mid-October.

At the **Island Cafe**, one block south of the ferry dock on Main Street, 747-6555, most of the dishes, such as pasta primavera, chicken, seafood, steak, barbecued ribs, sandwiches, and their famous island potatoes, are seasoned with herbs and spices. You can dine indoors, outdoors, or in-between on the screened porch. Open daily for breakfast, lunch, and dinner from May to mid-September and daily except Tuesday for lunch and dinner the rest of the year.

Mission Hill Coffee House, 105 Middle Rd., 747-3100, has fresh bakery and deli sandwiches besides gourmet coffee, espresso, and cappuccino. Open daily for breakfast, lunch, and dinner from late May to mid-October.

The Pub Restaurant, four blocks south of the ferry dock on Main Street, 747-6315, 800/822-6315, specializes in seafood but also has steak, salads, pasta, and sandwiches, including a great black bean burger and pepper steak sandwich. Start your meal with the focaccia (Italian flat bread covered with garlic, herbs, and mozzarella cheese). It also has creative daily specials and a good wine list. You can eat in the lakeside dining room or outdoor patio. Open daily for lunch and dinner from Memorial Day weekend to Labor Day; lunch is served only on Saturday and Sunday from early May to Memorial Day weekend and from Labor Day to mid-October.

Where to Stay

Most places will pick you up at the ferry dock, marina, or airport.

Bed-and-Breakfasts

Brittany Bed & Breakfast, 1.25 miles south of the ferry dock, 747-5023, was the island's first lodging establishment. The 1905 Adirondack camp–style houses, which have changed little over the years, are located on a lovely 12 acres on Lake Superior with formal gardens and private beach and dock. The estate has been nominated for listing on the National Register of Historic Places. The five antique-filled guest rooms each have private baths, all but one attached. There are also three cabins (two with two bedrooms) with kitchens and decks; one has a screened porch. A full breakfast is served in the dining room. Open Memorial Day weekend to mid-October.

Woods Manor, at the end of Nebraska Row, 747-3102, 800/WOODS-56, is a beautiful and fancy 1920s home with some Spanish influence. The house on five acres overlooking Lake Superior is located on Nebraska Row, where a wealthy circle of friends from Lincoln, Nebraska, built summer homes in the early 1900s. There are seven antique-filled guest rooms, including some Jacuzzi suites, with private baths. A few rooms have private balconies. Another three rooms are located nearby in the Carriage House and Northwoods Lodge. Guests have use of a pool, whirlpool, sauna, bicycles, and canoes and will enjoy a continental breakfast in the morning. Open May through December.

Other Lodging

The Inn on Madeline Island, four blocks south of the ferry dock on Main Street, 747-6315, 800/822-6315, adjacent to the marina, has 50 diverse units ranging from fancy one- and two-bedroom condos to comfortable two- and three-bedroom cottages to private homes around the island. Resort amenities include a beach, heated swimming pool, whirlpool, sauna, and clay tennis courts.

Island Inn, across from the ferry dock on Main Street, 747-2000, has five rooms.

Madeline Island Motel, 261 Colonel Woods Blvd., 747-3000, has 11 rooms, and guests receive a free continental breakfast.

The following businesses rent private homes and cottages around the island for short- or long-term stays: **Bog Lake Outfitters**, 747-2685; **Madeline Island Home Rentals**, 747-5135, 800/977-2624; and **Madeline Island Rentals**, 747-5775, 888/747-5775.

Camping is available at **Big Bay State Park** (p. 16) and **Big Bay Town Park** (p. 16).

Emergencies

Call 800/472-6927. The nearest hospital is in Ashland.

More Information

Madeline Island Chamber of Commerce, P.O. Box 274, La Pointe 54850, 747-2801, 888/ISLE-FUN, www.madelineisland.com. The chamber offices are one block south of the ferry dock at Middle Road, and there is a kiosk with information at the ferry landing in Bayfield.

Red Cliff Reservation

The 8,000-acre Red Cliff Reservation, created by the 1854 Treaty of La Pointe, hugs the northern tip of the scenic Bayfield Peninsula. Because of its central location it is known as the Hub of the Ojibwe Nation. The reservation was preceded by a small fishing village settled early in the nineteenth century, and fishing remains vital to the economy. The tribal-run Buffalo Bay Fish Company is a wholesale operation that purchases the catch from local fishermen.

Red Cliff is also the name of the reservation's only village. Originally called Buffalo Bay after Chief Buffalo, the principal chief of the Lake Superior band of Ojibwe at the time, the village was settled by Protestant Ojibwe while Catholic converts went to the Bad River Reservation (p. 65).

Today 857 people, mostly tribal members, call the reservation home, but you'd never know it from the small village since most people live scattered over a larger area. Though there isn't much in Red Cliff it does benefit from its proximity to Bayfield.

Things to See and Do

Isle Vista Casino has blackjack, slot machines, video poker and keno, and bingo for those 21 and older. Be sure to check out the 84-foot Mural of Indian Life that adorns the main gambling hall. There is an adjoining bar and restaurant, and the casino hosts frequent live entertainment. Located downtown on Hwy 13, 779-3712, 800/226-8478. Open daily. Wheelchair accessible.

The **Little Sand Bay Visitor Center** of the Apostle Islands National Lakeshore (p. 2) has historical displays, sells guidebooks, and provides visitor information. Also here are a boat launch and a beautiful beach. This is a convenient spot for kayak launch. Next door is the **Hokenson Brothers Fishery**, a restored commercial fishing operation from the first half of the century, now listed on the National Register of Historic Places. Even if you don't take the informative guided tour, there is plenty to see on your own. You can see the boats, nets, and dock and peer inside at the equipment in the restored buildings. Located two miles northwest of the casino on Hwy 13, four miles northwest on Hwy K, and 2.5 miles north on Little Sand Bay Road, 779-3397. Open 9–5 daily, Memorial Day weekend to Labor Day, and weekends in September. Tours of Hokenson Brothers Fishery at 10 and 2. Wheelchair accessible.

Events

The **Red Cliff Traditional Powwow**, held Fourth of July weekend, features dancing and drumming by performers in traditional dress from across the Midwest and Canada. You can also enjoy Native American food and arts and a fireworks display. $

Red Cliff Cultural Days, held in late July or early August in a traditional village erected behind the Isle Vista Casino, celebrates the history of the Ojibwe people. Visitors can observe or participate in storytelling, dancing, drumming, craft demonstrations, birchbark canoe making, a fish boil, and a traditional powwow.

Shopping

Native Spirit Gifts sells high-quality Native American art and gifts, jewelry, rugs and blankets, Wisconsin food items, and books. There are also some historical and cultural displays, including a birchbark wigwam where special events are occasionally held during the summer. Located on Hwy 13, 0.25 mile north of the casino, 779-9550. Open daily, Memorial Day weekend to early October, and then weekends through December.

Marinas/Charters

Buffalo Bay Marina, on Hwy 13 across from the casino, 779-3743, has 45 slips for seasonal and transient dockage.

Roys Point Marina, one mile south on Hwy 13, 779-5025, is a full service marina with 45 slips for transient and seasonal dockage.

You can take a sail on **Sandpiper**, a 35-foot classic wooden ketch, through the Thimbleberry Inn, 779-5757, 800/881-5903.

Where to Eat

The **Isle Vista Casino Restaurant**, attached to the casino (p. 20), 779-3712, 800/226-8478, serves value-priced family style meals including sandwiches, steaks, chicken, and pizza. Nightly specials include a Friday fish fry and Saturday prime rib. From late June to Labor Day weekend it also offers "Dining under the Pines," which is a fish boil on Fridays and sizzling steaks on Saturdays. Open daily for lunch and dinner plus breakfast on Saturday and Sunday.

Where to Stay

Bed-and-Breakfast

Thimbleberry Inn, 1.25 miles north of the casino on Blueberry Road then east to the end of Pageant Road, 779-5757, 800/881-5903, is a modern lakeside home on 40 wooded acres specially constructed to take in the fantastic island views with floor to ceiling windows. The three guest rooms have private baths, private entrances, and fireplaces. Enjoy a full gourmet breakfast on the deck or dining room, both with great views.

Other Lodging

The tribal-owned **Buffalo Bay Campground**, on Hwy 13 across from the casino, has 41 campsites, 12 with electric, on Lake Superior and showers. Open May to mid-October.

Point-Detour Campground, also operated by the Red Cliff Band, has 23 rustic sites in a beautiful wilderness setting on the far northern tip of mainland Wisconsin. You can follow the unmaintained trails above the cliffs, climb down and explore the rocky shoreline, or just take in the great Apostle Island and sunset views. It's worth a visit even if you don't plan to camp. Located two miles northwest of the casino on Hwy 13 then four miles northwest on Hwy K to Little Sand Bay Road where you can follow the signs 4.5 miles to the campground. Open May to mid-October.

The **Town of Russell Campground**, immediately across from the Little Sand Bay Visitor Center (p. 21), has 18 campsites, nine with electric. Open May to mid-October.

Emergencies

Call 373-6120. The nearest hospital is in Ashland.

More Information

Red Cliff Chamber of Commerce, P.O. Box 529, Bayfield 54814, 779-5225.

Washburn

People often drive right through Washburn on their way to Bayfield—in fact, there have long been discussions about adding traffic lights along Hwy 13 just to get people to stop. But those who do spend some time in this city of 2,321 overlooking Chequamegon Bay are sure to enjoy themselves. There are plenty of interesting things to see, and prices are much more reasonable than in Bayfield.

The county seat and largest community in Bayfield County, Washburn sprang up almost overnight in 1884 when it was founded by the Chicago, St. Paul, Minneapolis, and Omaha Railway as a sawmill and shipping center. It was named for Cadwallader Washburn, founder of the Washburn-Crosby Milling Firm, who had been a U.S. congressman and governor of Wisconsin. Soon a grain elevator and coal dock joined the city's three sawmills on the waterfront. Brownstone quarrying was also significant to Washburn's early success.

Though the timber companies logged themselves out of existence by the early 1900s and shipping faded, the economy exploded—literally—in 1905 when the DuPont Corporation opened the Barksdale Works explosive plant three miles south of town (you can still see the gated plant entrance and company homes along the highway). Barksdale produced explosives for the Lake Superior region's copper and iron mines, and when World War I broke out it became the world's largest producer of dynamite. After a long slowdown in production, operations ceased entirely in 1976.

With the founding industries gone the waterfront is now dominated by parks and a marina which support the city's new economic base: tourism.

Have County Seat, Will Travel

The city of Bayfield may be the center of tourism in Bayfield County, but Washburn has been the center of government since 1892 when the county seat was shifted here from Bayfield. Though Washburn was founded only in 1884 it grew rapidly and by 1892 had a population much greater than Bayfield's. That year a group of prominent Washburnites managed to get the issue of relocation put on the November ballot. After the election the residents of Bayfield couldn't feud with the numbers since the issue easily passed by a vote of 1,755 for the move and 1,147 against; they did, however, vigorously denounce the "unscrupulous maneuvering" and "political connivery" used to drum up support.

The "County Seat Ring," as the leading Washburn proponents became known, used both conventional and creative methods to persuade voters. They took out newspaper ads, distributed petitions, lobbied anyone who would listen, and even divided a five-acre plot of land into 25-foot lots and sold them for a dollar each to raise money. One time they chartered a train to a fair in Iron River, taking along a group of people to help decide a popularity contest being held between two women, one representing each side of the county seat issue. In the end it was estimated that the Ring had spent anywhere from ten to fifteen dollars per vote.

Iron River was another player in the debate. The *Iron River Times* editorialized that the county was still too young to make a final decision on the location and later claimed, "The true reason why a vote was taken on the county seat question was jealous fear on the part of Washburn of the growth and development of Iron River."

The very day that the governor signed the official decree people from Washburn went to Bayfield and in a matter of hours moved everything to their city. An attempt at serving a last-minute court injunction was thwarted when the county clerk, a Washburn supporter, hid in the attic of the Washburn Brewery until the injunction was no longer valid. Temporary offices were set up in the Washburn Town Hall until construction of a new county building could be completed in Washburn to replace the one built in Bayfield just nine years before.

The people of Bayfield really had no right to protest since they had successfully won a vote to move the county seat from La Pointe just 23 years before. That election resulted in the creation of the present Ashland and Bayfield Counties.

Things to See and Do

The **Washburn Museum and Cultural Center**, 1 E. Bayfield St., 373-5591, is located in the 1890 Bank of Washburn, a beautiful brownstone on the National Register of Historic Places. The historical displays include many old photos and turn-of the-century memorabilia; be sure to look at the old casket, washing machine, and wheelchair. The diorama of the waterfront circa 1900 shows how much has changed since then. The first floor hosts concerts, art shows, and classes and has a gift shop. In the summer months take a quick ride around town in an immaculate 1937 Oldsmobile. Work is under way on a hands-on children's science museum on the third floor. Located at 1 E. Bayfield St., 373-5591. Open 10–4, weekends in April and May, and most days from June to December. Wheelchair accessible.

Next to the museum is a 27-1/2-foot **obelisk** made of small brownstone blocks. The sculpture is a 1/4 scale model of the original 110-foot solid brownstone obelisk (five feet longer than the largest Egyptian obelisk) cut for, but never shipped to, the 1893 World's Fair in Chicago. The story is more interesting than the sculpture, but it's certainly worth a look.

The museum is just one of many historic buildings on Bayfield Street and elsewhere in town. Two other brownstones are listed on the National Register of Historic Places: the **Bayfield County Courthouse**, 117 E. Fifth St., is an 1894 Neo-Classical Revival building with a domed cupola, Roman-style pillars, and beautiful interior woodwork; the **Washburn Public Library**, 307 Washington Ave., is a 1904 Carnegie library.

The building isn't nearly as grand as the others, but you should stop by the **Washburn Iron Works** at 112 E. Bayfield St. to admire the exterior paintings.

Also worth a look on Bayfield Street is the 90-year-old **Lombardy poplar**, an 80-foot state champion tree located next to the Dairy Queen.

Washburn has two popular lakeshore parks. The more relaxing of the two is **Memorial Park** at the northeast end of town. It has 50 wooded campsites with electrical and cable TV hookups plus scenic shoreline views. **Thompson's West End Park**, at the end of Eighth Avenue, has 46 electric campsites plus a boat launch, fishing pier, and an artesian well. You'll find a beach, picnic area, playground, volleyball court, showers, and dump station at both parks. The campgrounds are open mid-April to mid-October.

Stretching between Thompson's Park and the marina is the one-mile **Lakeshore Walking Trail**. The historic path, used since logging days, was recently improved with bridges, a gravel base, and historical markers.

Many people come to **Big Rock County Park** on the Sioux River for the excellent fishing or just to watch the spring and fall spawning runs of trout and salmon. It's also a good wildlife viewing area and has 15 rustic campsites, a short but steep hiking trail, and a picnic area along Big Rock Ledges, which are scenic sandstone cliffs lining the river. Located 1.5 miles northwest on Hwy C then 1.5 miles north on Big Rock Road. Open April through October.

The **Chequamegon National Forest Washburn Ranger Station** can answer all your questions about forest activities (p. 48). Located at 113 E. Bayfield St., 373-2667 Voice/TTY. Open 7–4:30 Monday–Friday.

Several sites within the forest are located near Washburn. The **Mount Valhalla Recreation Area** is most popular as a winter destination with 11.5 miles of groomed cross-country ski trails, sledding hill, and a small chalet with indoor fire pit, but hikers, mountain bikers, horseback riders, and ATV-ers make use of the trails the rest of the year. Located eight miles west on Hwy C. $

The one-mile **Birch Grove Trail** at the Birch Grove Campground loops around quiet West Twin Lake. Located one mile south on Hwy 13, six miles west on Wannebo Road, and 3.25 miles north on FR 435.

The **Long Lake Picnic Ground** has a beach, picnic area, carry-in boat access, and a 1.2-mile hiking trail around the lake. You can also access the **BAMBA mountain-bike trail system** (p. 28) here. Located one mile south on Hwy 13 then six miles west on Wannebo Road. $

Local opinion holds that the region's best place to swim in Lake Superior is at the long sandy beach by the **mouth of the Sioux River**; unfortunately it's no secret and can be quite crowded. Located 4.25 miles north along Hwy 13 at Friendly Valley Road.

Continuing another 0.75 miles north on Hwy 13 brings you to **Bayview Town Park** with a less scenic but also less crowded beach.

Sioux River Canoe offers canoeing, kayaking, fishing, and backpacking trips throughout the Northwoods. Its Squaw Bay sea cave trips are one of the best bargains around. Either sign up for one of the regular trips or custom design your own adventure. Trips are available for all experience levels. Located at 1047 W. Bayfield St., 373-5912. Open daily, June through August, Monday–Saturday (and Sundays by reservation) the rest of the year. $

Scenic Drive

The **Moquah Barrens Auto Tour** leads through a pine barrens restoration in the Chequamegon National Forest (p. 48) west of town. The area is a haven for wildlife, especially sharp-tailed grouse and other birds, and has been designated a National Natural Landmark. There are two routes to choose from, one paved and one on well-maintained gravel roads. Pick up an informational booklet and map at the forest headquarters in town (p. 26).

Events

Activities during **Historic Brownstone Days**, held the last weekend in July, include a parade, quarry tours, 10K run, quilt show, flea market, and sidewalk sales.

Shopping

There are three antique stores in town. **The Old Hippie** and **The Wooden Sailor**, though separate businesses, share the same building, phone, and hours. Located at 18 W. Bayfield St., 373-2680. Open Tuesday–Saturday, May–October, irregular winter hours. Just down the street at 136 W. Bayfield is **The Washburn Antique Shoppe**, 373-0926. Open Wednesday–Saturday, May–September; irregular winter hours.

The **Apostle Islands Gallery** has nautically themed wood carvings, most of them carved by owner John Roglinske. The fun-to-browse building with a New England fishing village feel is itself a work of art. Located at 201 W. Bayfield St. No phone and no regular hours.

The **Chequamegon Book & Coffee Company** has a large and quality selection of used books, plus some new titles, and an adjoining coffee shop. Located at 2 E. Bayfield St., 373-2899. Open daily. May through December, and then closed on some midweek days the rest of the year.

Karlyn's Gallery, a Washburn institution for over 30 years, features watercolors by Karlyn and work by other artists, including pottery, jewelry, paintings, prints, plus a large selection of cookbooks. She also offers watercolor painting workshops. Located at 318 W. Bayfield St., 373-2922. Open daily.

You won't want to miss the **Wayward Wind Studio & Gallery**, the chaotic world of woodcarver Bill Vienneaux. Dozens of chain saw sculptures, most of them only half finished, are scattered about the yard, while inside is some really impressive work, like bed frames and rocking horses. Several other whittlers and chiselers set up shop in back each summer. Located "a smile south of Washburn" on Hwy 13, 373-2708. Open, as the sign says, "By chance or appointment. If I'm home . . . I'm open."

Marinas/Charters

The 150-slip **Washburn Marina**, 125 Central Ave., 373-5050, is a full service facility with transient dockage. Its 150-ton Travelift is the largest on Lake Superior.

Gitcheegummee Guide Service, based at Outdoor Allure Bait & Tackle, one mile south on Hwy 13, 373-0551, can take you fishing on Lake Superior or inland lakes and rivers.

If you'd prefer horsepower to wind power for sightseeing around the Apostle Islands, call **Top Gun Tours**, 373-5277. They can arrange a private tour in their custom 42-foot Fountain powerboat.

Bicycling

The marked 12-mile **BAMBA mountain-bike trail system** largely follows seldom used dirt roads through the Chequamegon National Forest (p. 48). Eventually you should be able to pick up maps at the chamber offices at 109 W. Bayfield St..

Outdoor Rentals

Sioux River Canoe (p. 26) rents canoes, kayaks, inner tubes, camping gear, snowshoes, and cross-country skis and can provide shuttle service.

Where to Eat

Cantina del Norte, 310 W. Bayfield St., 373-2850, has a small menu of Americanized Mexican favorites plus burgers. The bar is shaped like a boat and even has a figurehead at the bow. There is outdoor seating. Open daily for lunch and dinner.

It's a Small World Family Restaurant, 144 W. Bayfield St., 373-5177, is one of the state's most remarkable restaurants and a must for all visitors to Washburn. It features a rotating menu of weekly ethnic specials that span the globe: from the routine, such as Mexican and Italian to the unexpected, including Polynesian, Amish, Polish, Australian, Irish, and Colombian. The specials comprise not just entrees, but soups, salads, beverages, and desserts as well. The regular menu is no less diverse with Oriental stir-fry, fajitas, gyros, pesto, steak, seafood, soups, salads, and Washburn's famous "Oddball" burger. Special dietary options can be accommodated. They also offer cooking classes. Open daily for lunch and dinner plus breakfast on weekends.

Sandie's Log Cabin Restaurant, 905 W. Bayfield St., 373-5728, serves basic family fare plus fresh fish and daily specials. Breakfast is served any time. Out front is a "time tree" from 1779; the log's rings show its size at the time of important historical events. Open daily for breakfast, lunch, and dinner; in winter, dinner on weekends only.

The smells of the **Steak Pit**, 125 Harbor View Dr., 373-5492, will draw you in. Steaks and seafood make up most of the menu, but other options include pasta and chicken dinners. The dining room overlooks the lake and marina. Open daily for dinner.

Where to Stay

Bed-and-Breakfast

Pilgrim's Rest, five miles west on Hwy C then one mile south on Church Corner Road to Maple Hill Road, 373-2964, is a rustic home set amidst 10 wooded acres in the hills west of Washburn. Your suite includes a private bath with hot tub, living room, and entrance, plus you can watch a movie on your VCR or the distant wilderness views around you. Enjoy a full breakfast in the dining room.

Other Lodging

Redwood Motel and Chalets, 26 W. Bayfield St., 373-5512, has 18 rooms with cable TV; some rooms have kitchens.

Super 8 Motel, Harbor View Drive, 373-5671, 800/800-8000, overlooks the lake and marina. It has 35 rooms with cable TV, sauna, whirlpool, and free continental breakfast.

Washburn Motel, 800 W. Bayfield St., 373-5580, has six cozy (or tiny, depending on your perspective) cabins with cable TV.

Camping is available at **Memorial** and **Thompson's West End** parks (p. 25), **Big Rock County Park** (p. 26), and the **Chequamegon National Forest** (p. 48).

Emergencies

Call 373-6120. The nearest hospital is in Ashland.

More Information

Washburn Chamber of Commerce, P.O. Box 74, Washburn 54891, 373-5017, 800/253-4495, www.win.bright.net/~washburn. The chamber offices are at 109 W. Bayfield St.

Chapter 2
Endless Shores
Cornucopia, Herbster, Port Wing

The beauty and charm of the Bayfield area continue right along Lake Superior's south shore in the quiet villages of Cornucopia, Herbster, and Port Wing. These old fishing villages are famous for their expansive sandy beaches, breathtaking sunsets, and leisurely pace. This is quite possibly the most relaxing destination in the state. Highway 13, which hugs the shore between Cornucopia and the Bayfield county line, is an especially beautiful drive with many Lake Superior vistas.

Cornucopia

The name that Minneapolis lawyer T. J. Stevenson gave to the village he platted here in 1902 shows that he expected great things. Stevenson choose this location on Siskiwit Bay speculating that a rail line would soon arrive. Though the railroad took its bounty elsewhere the community still prospered by turning to the surrounding area's abundant resources.

At its peak two sawmills in Cornucopia handled the work from nine area lumber camps, and brownstone quarries operated nearby. Commercial fishing developed in the 1920s as the other industries died out. Fishing thrived until the 1950s when it quickly faded, due in large part to the invasion of Lake Superior by sea lampreys. Today just two boats still fish commercially out of Cornie, but the picturesque harbor has been reclaimed by shopkeepers and artisans who have converted the old fishing buildings into unique shops. After enjoying the harbor and lake, there are several things worth seeing inland too. More tourists discover Cornie every year, though it remains a quiet, wonderful place.

Ho Ho Ho!

If an enterprising group of Cornucopians had got their way in 1940, travelers would be stopping by the quaint village of North Pole, Wisconsin. When the U.S. Post Office turned down the request of Marchville, Wisconsin, to change its name to North Pole (the postmaster there hoped to make money canceling Christmas mail) because the name "had no geographical significance," the citizens of Cornucopia voted overwhelmingly to petition postal officials for the name since they were (and still are) the northernmost village in Wisconsin. Postal officials again said no, this time reasoning that if they approved this one they would have to allow a North Pole in every state.

Things to See and Do

St. Mary's Orthodox Church is topped by a green onion-shaped cupola and many three-armed Russian Orthodox crosses. The church was built in 1910 by the area's numerous Slavic immigrants and was the first church erected in Cornucopia. It is still used by a small congregation. The hill behind the church is known as Gold Hill, for a local legend of bank robbers and buried treasure. Located at the south end of Erie Avenue.

East of the harbor is **Siskiwit Bay Park** with an artesian well, picnic area, playground, volleyball court, and a long sandy beach. Next to the park is a state historical marker about the Tragedy of Siskiwit, a legendary massacre of the Ojibwe by the Fox. If this area is too crowded the beach continues on the other side of the river.

Siskiwit Falls drops over a long series of short steps; it almost looks manmade. Take Hwy C 0.25 mile east of downtown to Siskiwit Falls Road. From the bridge a narrow path leads downstream to the main falls. A few hundred feet upstream from the bridge, also reachable by a narrow path, is another falls, just a little smaller than the main one, but not quite as beautiful.

Lost Creek Falls, about 15 feet tall, takes a lot more effort to reach, but it's well worth it. The remote falls can be difficult to find and there are several approaches to it, so you are advised to ask someone in town to show you the way on a map. There has been talk of marking a trail to it, but many locals are opposed so it's unlikely to happen.

The far west end of the **Apostle Islands National Lakeshore** (p. 2), at the end of Myer's Road, has an unbelievably beautiful sandy beach perfect for hiking. This is a popular departure point for kayakers since the Squaw Bay sea caves are located just to the east of here. Though best appreciated from the water, the caves can also be seen from the end of a rugged two-mile hiking trail that begins here. In winter, when frozen waterfalls form giant pillars and ice crystals form needle-like icicles, the caves are an incredible sight. The ice is generally safe for travel from late January until mid-March, but you should always check the ice conditions with the park service before heading out. Located four miles east on Hwy 13.

In the winter you can arrange **dog sledding trips** through Lazy Susan's B&B, 742-3443. **$**

Events

During **Cornucopia Day**, held the second Saturday in August, there is a parade, flea market, bake sale, sand castle building contest, street dance, games, and more.

Shopping

The five harbor shops have an eclectic mix of items that could best be described as a little of this and a little of that. Here's a brief description of each: **Art & Sol**, 742-3406, a variety of art, plus hand-woven clothes, some organic foods, and renewable energy information; **The Good Earth Shop,** 742-3910, a wide range of gifts, plus books and food; **River's End**, 742-3220, antiques and organic produce; **Sea Hag**, 779-5456, gifts, clothes, and antiques; **What Goes 'Round**, 742-3220, a large selection of used books, plus antiques and vintage clothes. Store owners don't keep regular hours, but if the tourists are here, they will be too. As a rough guide, they open in May—weekends at first, then daily during peak months—and stay open as long as the weather holds out.

For over 80 years **Ehler's Store**, an old-fashioned general store, has sold most everything anyone in Cornucopia would likely need including groceries, hardware, and clothes. Located just south of Hwy 13 on Superior Avenue, 742-3232. Open daily.

Marinas/Charters

Bell Marina, 742-3994, has 35 slips for short- and long-term docking.

Siskiwit Bay Marina, 742-3337, is a full service, 40-slip marina with short- and long-term docking.

Fish Lipps, 742-3378, offered charter fishing in the past and may do so again in the future.

You can arrange a Lake Superior sailing trip through **Lazy Susan's B&B**, 742-3443.

Where to Eat

The highly regarded **Village Inn**, at the junction of Hwys 13 and C, 742-3941, specializes in seafood (you can sample whitefish livers here) and offers other equally scrumptious options, such as steaks, roast duck, pastas, and prime rib on Saturday. Enjoy a fish boil in an outdoor screened pavilion on Friday and Saturday nights, June through October, by reservation. Open daily for lunch; dinner daily, June through October and Friday–Sunday the rest of the year.

Where to Stay

Bed-and-Breakfasts

Fo'c'sle Bed & Breakfast, 742-3337, has two guest rooms on the waterfront at Siskiwit Bay Marina with private attached baths, gas fireplaces, and private entry. A full breakfast is served in your room.

Lazy Susan's, 0.5 mile east on Hwy 13, 0.5 mile north on Squaw Point-W, and 0.25 mile west on Jack Pine Drive/Sun Set Road, 742-3443, is a large modern home with a rustic touch just outside town on a quiet 8.5 wooded acres fronting Lake Superior. The guest rooms, including a Jacuzzi suite, have private baths, gas fireplaces, and private decks. All have sunset views of Lake Superior. A continental breakfast is followed by a full brunch.

Other Lodging

Deerings Tourist Homes, on Hwy 13 across from the marina, 742-3994, have three small, simple cottages straight out of the 1950s with kitchens and fireplaces. Sometimes they take guests out for a sail.

South Shore Motel, at Hwy 13 and Superior Avenue, 742-3244, has 10 rooms overlooking the lake.

Swenson's Cottages, just south of town on Siskiwit Falls Road, 742-3282, are along Siskiwit Falls and a natural rock slide into the river. The four simple cottages have kitchens.

The Village Inn, at the junction of Hwys 13 and C, 742-3941, has four rooms and a comfortable sitting room with a fireplace and balcony where you can relax and enjoy a free continental breakfast in the morning.

Emergencies

Call 373-6120. The nearest hospital is in Ashland.

More Information

Cornucopia Business Association, P.O. Box 316, Cornucopia 54827, 742-3337.

Herbster

Blink and you'll miss it. Herbster is tiny and quiet, even compared with Cornucopia and Port Wing. The village was named after William Herbster, the cook for the Cranberry Lumber Company's camp located here. This honor was likely bestowed upon him because he was one of the few men in the camp who could read the lumberjacks' letters to them. The long sandy shore leading west of town toward the mouth of the Cranberry River is arguably the most scenic beach for strolling in the "endless shores" area.

Things to See and Do

Though log buildings aren't unusual in northern Wisconsin **The Gym** is worth a look just for its size. The WPA built this large structure in 1940, and it was used as a gymnasium until the local school was closed. It is currently being restored and is worth a peek inside to see the hardwood floor. It now serves primarily as Clover Town Hall and the Herbster Community Center. Occasionally dances are held here. Located on Lenawee Road, two blocks south of Hwy 13.

Clover Town Park on Lake Superior has a sandy beach, picnic area, and 30 campsites. Tent sites are right on the lake while RV sites with electricity are just across the road. There is a playground just down the street. Open May through September.

Take Bark Point Road 2.5 miles northeast to Bark Bay Road to drive through the **Bark Bay Slough State Natural Area**, a 225-acre bay and bog that harbors many rare plants and abundant wildlife. A boat landing 1.75 miles south on Bark Bay Road gives paddlers easy access to this quiet, scenic area as well as offering great views from land. You can also follow Bark Point Road to the boat launch at the end of Bark Point to enjoy the shoreline views.

Shopping

At the **Cabin Fever Quilt Company and Gift Shop**, you can see the "artistic picture quilts" created by Connie Daniel. She specializes in wildlife and nature scenes, but these beautiful and intricate works of art can also be custom made from your photos. There is also a small selection of pottery and crafts. Located just east of town on Bark Point Road, 774-3309, 888/774-3415. Open daily, May through October.

Northern Lights Gifts & Crafts carries locally made craft items, including machine-made quilts that can be custom made on short notice. There is also a book exchange. Located in town on Hwy 13, 774-3427. Open daily, mid-May to mid-October, and then weekends through December.

Orchard City Gift Shop is a small shop with a variety of craft and gift items. Antiques are for sale in the small building next door. Located in town on Hwy 13, 774-3812. There are no regular hours but it is open most days from Memorial Day weekend to Labor Day and weekends through October.

Where to Eat

The friendly **Cranberry Inn**, in town on Hwy 13, 774-3557, serves up tasty Italian dishes such as mostaccioli, ravioli, and pizza, as well as burgers. Open Tuesday–Sunday for dinner.

Where to Stay

Bed-and-Breakfast

The **Bark Point Inn**, just east of town on Bark Point Road, 774-3309, 888/774-3415, is a simple home overlooking Lake Superior. The one guest room (they plan to expand) has a private entrance and bath with a double whirlpool tub. In winter dozens of deer are fed in the yard. Enjoy a creative full breakfast in the dining room or on the deck.

Other Lodging

Lakeshore camping is available at **Clover Town Park** (p. 35).

Emergencies

Call 373-6120. The nearest hospital is in Ashland.

More Information

Herbster Community Club, P.O. Box 71, Herbster 54844, 774-3411.

Port Wing

Port Wing holds a notable distinction in state history. In 1903 the growing village formed the first consolidated school district in Wisconsin. The Port Wing school replaced several scattered one-room schools largely serving the children of lumberjacks. To get the children to the distant school the community organized horse-drawn wagons and sleighs, known as school rigs, thus creating the state's first public school bus.

The community that would become Port Wing got its start in 1891 when Axel Johannson settled at the natural harbor at the mouth of the Flag River after having sailed along the south shore from Duluth. It was named for Colonel Isaac Wing, a prominent Bayfield County lumberman.

Things to See and Do

If your kids complain about the bus ride to school, just stop by **Old School Memorial Park** and show them the replica of the canvas-covered wagon the kids around Port Wing rode to school in the early 1900s. Other interesting historical displays in the park include the old Port Wing jail, an early mail sled, a state historical marker, and a gazebo made from the bell tower of the old Port Wing School. There is also a picnic area and playground. Located in the center of town on Hwy 13.

On the west edge of town on Hwy 13 is **Twin Falls Park**. Follow the trail upstream about 1/4 mile to the overlook of the beautiful 15-foot double falls on Larson Creek. There is a small picnic area at the park entrance.

Orienta Falls is just a short series of rapids below a dam, but the steep, rocky gorge along the Iron River makes this a worthwhile stop. A short, steep, and rough trail (be careful here) leads to the river. Located five miles west of Port Wing: take Orienta Falls Road south of Hwy 13 for one mile and park where the road bends.

Events

The town's big event is the **Port Wing Fish Boil and Fall Festival**, held each Labor Day weekend. The self-proclaimed "world's largest fish boil" is held on Saturday; the Fall Festival on Sunday includes an arts and crafts fair, flea market, live music, fun run/walk, and parade. $ for fish boil.

Shopping

Country Treasures has a small selection of locally made crafts including some beautiful quilts. Located at 83260 Washington Ave., 774-3632. Open daily, May through early October, and at least some weekends through December.

Port Wing Pottery and Gallery offers work from 20 local artists in a quaint century-old Catholic church. Besides pottery, there are paintings, weavings, carved wooden chests, and more. You can also watch owner Shane Upthegrove create her pottery right here. Located in town on Hwy 13, 774-3222. Open daily during the summer; there are no set winter hours, but Shane is here most days and if there's a car in the parking lot, she says you're welcome to come in.

Marinas/Charters

Port Wing Marina, 9110 Beach Rd., 774-3555, is a full service marina with 38 slips for long- and short-term docking.

For Lake Superior charter fishing call **Day-O Charters**, 774-3354; **Northern Lite Charters**, 774-3673; **South Shore Charters**, 774-3555; or **Spoon Feeder Charters**, 774-3527.

Where to Eat

The homemade meals at the **Cottage Cafe**, kitty-corner from School Memorial Park on Hwy 13, 774-3565, include sandwiches, pizza, and daily specials such as steak and seafood. Open daily for breakfast, lunch, and dinner, but closed Wednesdays during the winter.

Where to Stay

Bed-and-Breakfast

The **Garden House**, 9255 Sunnyside Ln., 774-3705, is a simple country home on five acres with gardens and flowers. The one guest room has its own private bath, lounge, and entrance. Guests enjoy a creative full breakfast in the morning. Children are welcome.

Other Lodging

Anchor Inn Campground, at the junction of Hwys 13 and A, 774-3658, has eight RV campsites with full hookups and showers plus three simple cabins. Open mid-April to mid-October.

Holiday Pines Resort, 9135 Harbor Rd., 774-3555, has four rustic cabins with kitchens across from the marina. The two larger cabins have two bedrooms and fireplaces.

Emergencies

Call 373-6120. The nearest hospital is in Ashland.

More Information

Iron River Area Chamber, P.O. Box 448, Iron River 54847, 372-8558, www.iracc.com.

Chapter 3
Forest Primeval
Cable, Drummond, Iron River

Cable

Cable is the antithesis of Hayward, its southerly neighbor. You won't find any traffic jams or tourist traps in this small but lively village. The forests and waterways surrounding Cable make this area a mecca for silent sports lovers—bikers and cross-country skiers in particular. It seems as if every other vehicle has a bike or ski rack attached to it. In fact, Cable was recently recognized for its outstanding outdoor recreation when it was named a charter "Trail Town USA" by the American Hiking Society.

Cable was founded in 1880 when the Chicago, St. Paul, Minneapolis, and Omaha Railway arrived and was named for the first locomotive engineer to pull a train into town. Hundreds of railroad workers settled in this boom town as they continued to push the line north. There were many lumberjacks in the surrounding camps too and the town gained a reputation for rowdiness. Once the tracks reached Ashland there was an exodus of railroad construction crews, who constituted much of the population. The town also endured a devastating fire that had destroyed all of the makeshift saloons, stores, hotels, and houses. Those who remained rebuilt, and the town has survived with an economy supported almost entirely by tourism.

Things to See and Do

The **Cable Natural History Museum** hosts regularly changing exhibits and artwork focusing on the ecology of the Northwoods. The museum also has a hands-on children's area and a collection of animal mounts. The museum hosts a summer lecture series, junior naturalist programs, and field trips, such as full moon hikes and wildflower walks, that get you outdoors. The friendly staff will try to answer all your questions. Located on Hwy M, two blocks east of U.S.

63, 798-3890. Open 10–4 Tuesday–Saturday year-round plus 10–2 Sunday in July and August. Wheelchair accessible.

Connected to the museum is the historic **Forest Lodge Library** in a classic 1925 log building with a fieldstone fireplace.

The museum also maintains the **Forest Lodge Nature Trail**, which has three loops totaling 3.6 miles through several different ecological communities. An interpretive guide booklet is available at the museum or the trailhead. Located 8.5 miles east on Hwy M then one mile northeast on Garmisch Road.

Highlights of the nearby **Chequamegon National Forest** (p. 48) include the 13.6-mile **Rock Lake National Recreation Trail** with several loops through a beautiful forest surrounding several lakes. The western half is in a semiprimitive nonmotorized area. It is one of the area's more popular and challenging mountain biking and cross-country skiing trails. The nearest trailhead is eight miles east on Hwy M. $

Lynch Creek is a remote and wonderful area: great for viewing wildlife, including nesting bald eagles. A 0.25-mile trail leads to a viewing platform overlooking the north end of a small flowage, and a half-mile trail leads along the flowage's south shore. Located 10 miles east on Hwy M, 4.5 miles south on FR 203, and 0.3 mile south on FR 622.

The three-mile **Namekagon Trail** has three easy loops (one of which has an interpretive guide booklet available at the trailhead) totaling three miles. It is groomed for cross-country skiing in the winter. Located across from the Namekagon Campground, 11 miles east on Hwy M, 5.5 miles north on Hwy D, and 0.3 miles west on FR 209.

The Namekagon River, part of the **St. Croix National Scenic Riverway** (p. 136), can be accessed at the wayside 1.5 miles south on U.S. 63. Water levels here are usually suitable for canoeing only through midsummer.

Before it closed, winter enthusiasts flocked to **Telemark Resort** for downhill skiing and snowboarding on Mount Telemark's 10 runs. There were also 65 km of cross-country ski trails, including part of the famous **Birkebeiner Trail**. There is a good chance it will reopen with new owners. Located two miles east on Hwy M then two miles south on Telemark Road. $

Scenic Drive

Several different marked **Fall Color Tours** (beautiful any time of the year) lead through the surrounding forest. You can pick up a map of the routes at the Cable Area Visitor Center.

CAMBA

The Chequamegon Area Mountain Bike Association (CAMBA) has marked and mapped over 300 miles of trails in and around the Chequamegon National Forest (p. 48), creating one of the nation's premier off-road bike trail systems. Ranging from quiet country roads to extreme single track, it offers something for everyone, whether a leisurely ride with young children or a limit-testing challenge. And, with this many miles of trail to choose from, you won't find any crowds, no matter how far you ride. The well-marked trails are grouped into six clusters stretching between Hayward and Iron River, and most are ridable from May through November. To get additional information or current trail conditions or to purchase maps, contact CAMBA, P.O. Box 141, Cable 54821, or the Cable Area Chamber of Commerce, P.O. Box 217, Cable 54821, 800/533-7454.

Events

The **American Birkebeiner**, held in late February, is the nation's largest cross-country skiing race, attracting around 8,000 skiers and more than three times that many spectators. Racers taking on the 52 km course from the Telemark Resort to Hayward (the finish line is on Main Street) include the world's top skiers plus weekend warriors just looking for personal glory. The big event is preceded by children's and family fun races, elite sprints, the 25 km Kortelopet race, winter sports equipment demos, and an Olympics-style opening ceremony.

The **Chequamegon Fat Tire Festival**, held the second weekend after Labor Day, is one of the nation's premier off-road bike races and the largest of the many mountain-biking events held here. The main race is the Chequamegon 40, which runs from Hayward to Telemark Resort, where most activities are based. Some of the other events include the Short and Fat 16, Rough Stuff Rendezvous orienteering event, Cable Criterium lap race, children's bicycle parade and rodeo, klunker toss, and a hill climb. The 2,500 highly coveted racing slots are granted by lottery. Call 798-3811 for details.

Shopping

Cottage Shop Antiques is located in a simple log cabin built in the 1930s and has a huge selection of old lamps. Located two miles east on Hwy M, 798-3077. Open daily except Wednesday from Memorial Day weekend through October.

Right next door, surrounded by dozens of old boats, is **Nordik Sleigh Antique Shop**, 798-3967. It also has many crafts and wood sculptures made on site. Open most days May through October, by chance or appointment the rest of the year.

Cranberry Max has high-quality art and gift items plus some rustic furniture. Located one mile south on U.S. 63, 798-3332. Open daily, mid-May through September.

The Gallery features artwork from many regional artists including woodwork, glasswork, basketry, and painting. A showroom here features the popular work of Blue Moon Pottery . You'll also find gourmet foods, custom framing, and the Christmas Shoppe. Located at the corner of Hwy M and Main Street, 798-3133. Open daily, May through December, and reduced hours the rest of the year.

Honey Creek Antiques has a small but quality selection. Located 2.5 miles south on U.S. 63, 798-3958. Open daily except Wednesday.

Oldies But Goodies is the only antique store right in town. Located on Main Street half a block south of Hwy M, 798-4904. Open Wednesday–Saturday, May through October, and Friday–Saturday, November through April.

Golf

There are three area golf courses to choose from: **Forest Ridges Golf Course**, eight miles east on Hwy M at Lakewoods Resort, 794-2698, has 18 holes; **Tahkodah Hills Golf Course**, 2.75 miles east on Hwy M then 2.75 miles north on Lake Owen Drive, 798-3760, has 9 holes; **Telemark Golf Course**, two miles east on Hwy M then two miles south on Telemark Road, 798-3104, has 18 holes.

Bicycling

Cable is right at the heart of the **CAMBA trail system** (p. 42).

Outdoor Rentals

Big Brook Bait & Laundromat, 0.5 mile south on U.S. 63, 798-3310, rents canoes and kayaks and offers a shuttle service.

Lakeside Lawn & Sport, U.S. 63 and Hwy M, 798-3030, rents snowmobiles.

Lakewoods Resort, 8.25 miles east on Hwy M, 794-2561, 800/255-5937, rents canoes, kayaks, fishing boats, pontoons, and snowmobiles.

Where to Eat

B & B Cafe, on U.S. 63 on the south edge of town, 798-3003, has basic diner fare served fast and cheap. Try the homemade soups. Open Monday–Saturday for breakfast and lunch and Sunday for breakfast.

Garmisch Inn Restaurant and Lounge, eight miles east on Hwy M then 1.75 miles northeast on Garmisch Road, 794-2204, 800/794-2204, serves fine German and American fare with many steak and seafood dishes and several different schnitzels. Some of the more interesting menu options are honey fried chicken and cranberry peppercorn pork. There is an all-you-can-eat fish fry on Friday. Along with the great food comes an incredible setting overlooking Lake Namekagon with outdoor seating and an extensive wine list. Open daily for breakfast, lunch, and dinner.

Nadine's Backwoods Bistro, at the junction of U.S. 63 and Hwy M, 798-4900, has a small but creative menu with unique options such as Greek pizza, Cajun chicken wrap, teriyaki shrimp, chicken curry, plus steak, seafood, pasta, sandwiches, and a salad bar. Nightly specials include prime rib on Wednesday and Saturday and a Friday fish fry. Nadine's has the only full bar in the village. Open daily for breakfast, lunch, and dinner.

Where to Stay

Bed-and-Breakfast

Connors of Cable, one mile north on U.S. 63 then 0.25 mile east on Birch Lane, 798-3661, 800/848-3932, occupies 77 acres of what was once a farm. There are four guest rooms, two with private attached baths plus two shared baths. One suite has a whirlpool and fireplace and each room has satellite TV. Also available is an 1890s log cabin with kitchen in the apple orchard. Sports enthusiasts benefit from the ski waxing and bike repair area. Guests are served a full breakfast in the dining room.

Other Lodging

Alpine Resort Motel, 1.5 miles east on Hwy M, two miles north on Trail Inn Road, and 0.75 miles west on Resort Road, 798-3603, 800/872-9370, has 12 motel rooms, including some suites and kitchenettes, on Lake Owen with whirlpool, sauna, rec room, beach, boat and pontoon rentals, and a snack shop. Here your aquatic enjoyment is not limited to the surface of the water since they offer scuba diving.

Bon Nuit l'Hotel, on Main Street one block north of Hwy M, 798-3792, 800/266-6848, has 11 rooms with cable TV. This is the only lodging downtown.

Garmisch USA, eight miles east on Hwy M then 1.75 miles northeast on Garmisch Road, 794-2204, 800/794-2204, is "a Bavarian paradise in the Northwoods." This incredible resort has creative old world–style buildings on 55 acres on Lake Namekagon. Each of the 12 one- to five-bedroom cottages (including a castle!) has its own kitchen and fireplace. There are also seven rooms and a whirlpool suite in the beautiful 1920s main lodge, most with their own fireplace and some with kitchens. Boats are available for guest use and pontoons are available for rent. Other resort amenities include a beach, tennis courts, game room, restaurant, and bar.

King's Lodge, two miles north on U.S. 63, one mile northwest on Blue Moon Road, and one mile west on Tri-Lakes Road, 798-4888, is a restored classic 1930s Northwoods lodge on quiet Lake Wilipyro that caters to silent sports enthusiasts: "snowmobiles not invited." The six cabins range from one to five bedrooms and include a rowboat and private dock. Guests can also enjoy the wood-fired Finnish sauna and beach.

Lakewoods Resort, 8.25 miles east on Hwy M, 794-2561, 800/255-5937, is a large resort on Lake Namekagon with something for everybody. There are 33 motel rooms, including several whirlpool suites, plus 22 cottages and 46 condos ranging from one to four bedrooms. All cottages and condos have kitchens, fireplaces, and private decks or balconies, and some have whirlpools. The resort has an indoor and outdoor pool, whirlpool, sauna, beach, game room, restaurant/bar, tennis and volleyball courts, and a golf course. Boats and pontoons are available for rent, and some rental units include a boat. *Snowgoer* magazine called this the top snowmobile resort in the country.

The **Pilot Fish Inn**, two miles east on Hwy M then 0.25 mile south on Telemark Road, 798-3474, has eight rooms, some with kitchens and satellite TV, and two suites. They also provide videos and plush terry robes.

Recreation Rental Properties, based at the Pioneer Bar, 11 miles east on Hwy M then six miles north on Hwy D, 794-2622, rents fully equipped houses on several area lakes.

Telemark Resort, two miles east on Hwy M then two miles south on Telemark Road, is Wisconsin's premier winter resort with a downhill ski area and an extensive cross-country ski trail system. Though winter is its specialty, this complete four-season facility also has great golf and mountain biking. There are 200 lodge rooms, including luxury whirlpool suites, and 58 condos. Among the countless resort facilities are indoor and outdoor pool; whirlpool; sauna; masseuse; basketball, tennis, volleyball, and badminton courts; and a game room. There is a restaurant/bar, and guests enjoy a free continental breakfast. You can even fly in since the Cable Airport is located here. At this writing, ownership and status of the Telemark Resort were in doubt. For current information call the Cable Area Chamber of Commerce, 798-3833, 800/533-7454.

Camping is available in the **Chequamegon National Forest** (p. 48).

Emergencies

Call 373-6120. The nearest hospital is in Hayward.

More Information

Cable Area Chamber of Commerce, P.O. Box 217, Cable 54821, 798-3833, 800/533-7454, www.cable4fun.com. The Cable Area Visitor Center is located one block east of U.S. 63 on Hwy M.

Drummond

Drummond was a company town created and owned by the Rust-Owen Lumber Company, which operated a mill here from 1883 to 1930, and many of the original houses built for the workers still stand. This quiet village lies in the Chequamegon National Forest (p. 48) and logging remains a major employer with the Aspen Lumber Company located right in the center of town.

Things to See and Do

The **Drummond Historical Museum** traces the logging history of the town with displays of old tools, household items, and photographs. There is also an interesting wildlife exhibit of native Northwoods animals. The museum is located in the library at Superior Street and Owen Avenue, 739-6290. Open 12:30–5:30 Tuesday, 10–2 Wednesday, 11–6 Thursday, 10–2 Saturday. Wheelchair accessible.

Another historic site in town is the **Rust-Owen Reservoir**, one of the last remnants of the mill that brought the town into existence. Most of the massive circular fieldstone base remains atop a hill overlooking the town. The basin could hold 180,000 gallons of water and twice prevented fires from destroying the town. It's not worth going out of your way to see, but if you're here you may want to stop. A historical brochure is provided at the trailhead. Located 0.5 mile north on Delta-Drummond Road at the end of a short trail.

In the surrounding **Chequamegon National Forest** (p. 48) you will find several excellent trails. The **North Country National Scenic Trail** (p. 98) passes through the forest's two wilderness areas, both of which are near town. The 6,600-acre **Rainbow Lake Wilderness Area**, one of the first official wilderness areas east of the Mississippi River, is four miles north on Delta-Drummond Road. The 4,450-acre **Porcupine Lake Wilderness Area** is six miles southeast on Lake Owen Drive (FR 213).

The one-mile **Drummond Woods Interpretive Trail**, which shares part of its path with the North Country National Scenic Trail, passes through an old growth white pine forest and has historical and ecological markers along its path. Located one mile northeast on U.S. 63 at the intersection of Old 63 North (FR 235).

The **Drummond Trail**, has several loops totaling 10.5 miles. It is a popular off-road biking and cross-country skiing trail. Located one mile south on Lake Owen Drive (FR 213). $

The 1.5-mile **Bass Lake Interpretive Trail**, at the Two Lakes Campground, loops around Bass Lake. Located five miles southeast on Lake Owen Drive.

Also in the forest is the **Pigeon Lake Interpretive Trail**, maintained by the University of Wisconsin at its Pigeon Lake Field Station, a facility used primarily by students and other groups for outdoor education. Interpretive signs discuss the various forest communities and small bog lake the 1.3-mile loop passes through. Located three miles west on Hwy N then one mile north on Pigeon Lake Road.

The **White River**, which snakes through the **Bibon Swamp State Natural Area**, one of the state's largest wetlands, is a popular canoe route. It is a great place for fly fishing and birdwatching and is the area's best bet for late-season paddling. Bear Country Sporting Goods (see Outdoor Rentals) can provide you with all the information you need to enjoy this beautiful area.

Bicycling

There is easy access to the **CAMBA trail system** (p. 42).

Outdoor Rentals

Bear Country Sporting Goods, at the intersection of U.S. 63 and Wisconsin Avenue, 739-6645, rents canoes, boats, and pontoons and offers a shuttle service.

CAMPGROUND	CAMP SITES	WALKIN SITES	WHEELCHAIR ACCESSIBLE	DUMP STATION	SWIMMING BEACH	RESERVATION
1. Beaver Lake	10					
2. Birch Grove	16					
3. Black Lake	29	3	•		•	A
4. Day Lake	52	1	•		•	A
5. East Twin	10		•			
6. Lake Three	8					
7. Mineral Lake	11				•	
8. Moose Lake	15				•	A
9. Namekagon	33		•			A
10. Perch Lake	16					
11. Stockfarm Bridge	8					
12. Two Lakes	90	7	•	•	•	B
13. Wanoka Lake	20					

Chequamegon National Forest

From remote backpacking journeys to leisurely auto tours, week-long paddling trips to picnic lunches at developed facilities, there is something for everyone in the Chequamegon (sheh-wau-meh-gahn). The forest has over 860,000 acres in three separate sections, the largest and wildest of which is spread out across the area covered by this guidebook. Over two dozen trails, wilderness areas, scenic drives, recreation areas, historic sites, and other facilities are detailed with the nearest community.

With its vast size and myriad of habitats it's no surprise that wildlife abounds in the forest. Over 225 species of birds and most of the state's mammals can be spotted here. Timber wolf, pine marten, bald eagle, osprey, peregrine falcon, red-shouldered hawk, and great egret, all threatened or endangered species, are some of the most thrilling sightings. Other rare or exciting animals found here include common loon, bear, bobcat, otter, fisher, and badger. If you're really lucky you might even spot an elk (p. 72).

For more information about the forest, contact one of the district ranger offices in Glidden (p. 71), Hayward (p. 108), or Washburn (p. 26) or Forest Supervisor, 1170 Fourth Ave. South, Park Falls 54552, 762-2461.

Camping in Chequamegon National Forest

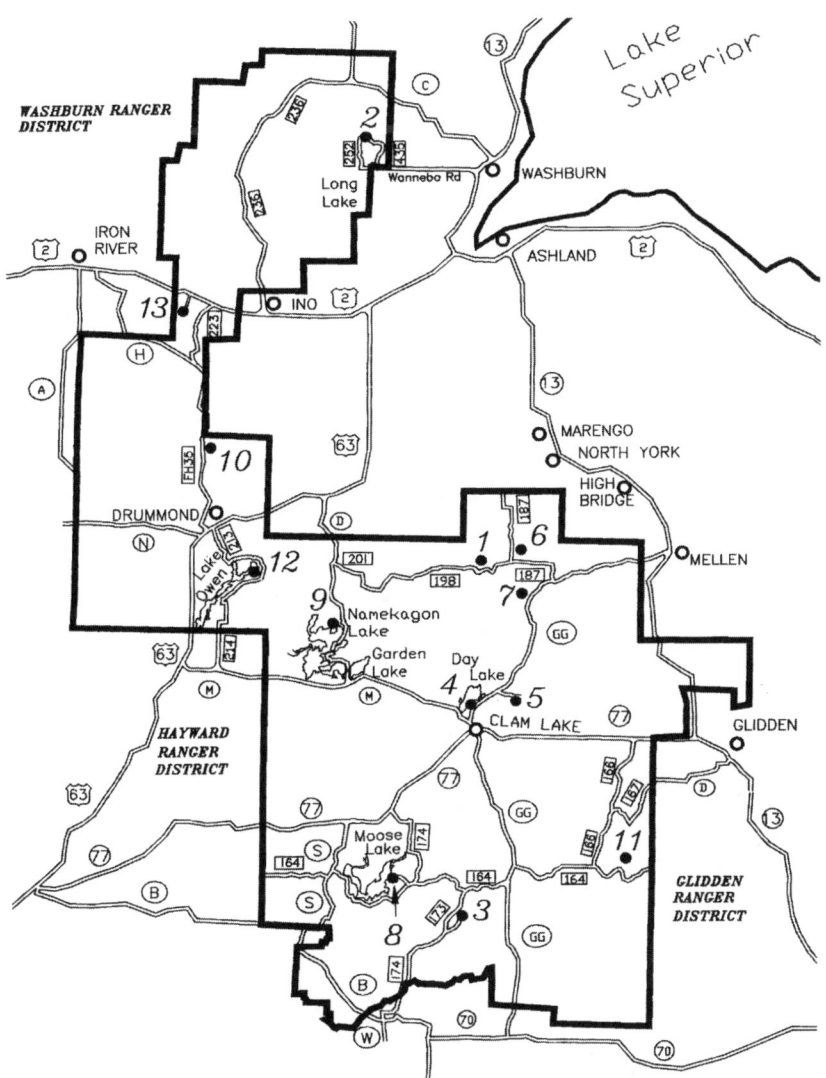

A Call 264-2511, **B** Call 739-6334. These also have first-come, first-served sites.

The campgrounds are officially open May through October. Winter camping is allowed, but facilities are not maintained and only Day Lake is plowed.

Where to Eat

Black Bear Inn, U.S. 63 and Wisconsin Avenue, 739-6313, serves sandwiches, salads, Italian specialties, steak, seafood, and fried chicken. The Friday night fish fry features fresh Lake Superior whitefish and trout. Open daily for lunch and dinner.

Where to Stay

Bed-and-Breakfasts

Chequamegon House, just south of town at the junction of U.S. 63 and Hwy N, 739-6665, is a simple rustic home surrounded on both levels by decks. There are eight guest rooms, some with private baths; the "economy" rooms with shared baths are a bargain. It offers a continental breakfast and a TV and VCR in the community room.

Hummingbird B&B, four miles north on Hwy 27 then half a mile east on S. Sweden Road, 763-3214, is named for the pint-size feathered friends that share this quiet 70-acre country getaway with you. There are two guest rooms with shared baths and one suite with private bath and sitting room. The common room has games and a TV with VCR, and there is also a bike and ski work and storage area. Enjoy a full breakfast and an evening dessert in the dining room or screened porch.

Other Lodging

Black Bear Motel, U.S. 63 and Wisconsin Avenue, 739-6313, has four simple rooms.

Camping is available in the **Chequamegon National Forest** (p. 48).

Emergencies

Call 373-6120. The nearest hospital is in Hayward.

More Information

Cable Area Chamber of Commerce, P.O. Box 217, Cable 54821, 798-3833, 800/533-7454, www.cable4fun.com.

Iron River

Iron River is a small town straddling U.S. 2 (called Mill Street downtown) about halfway between Superior and Ashland. There are some interesting sites and shops that draw in many people just passing through town. Originally called Medicine Springs by the Ojibwe who traveled here for the supposed health benefits, the town quickly filled with loggers when established in 1887. The rail line between Ashland and Hurley was kept busy shipping the lumber cut at the town's sawmill. Many Scandinavian settlers took up farming after the forests were cleared and many of their descendants remain. Iron River became known as the blueberry capital of the world, thanks to an abundance of this little fruit.

Things to See and Do

The **Western Bayfield County Historical Museum** houses an interesting collection of turn-of-the-century artifacts, including household items, logging tools, farm equipment, medical instruments, clothing, and much more. The friendly hosts will be happy to share some stories from Iron River's early days. The museum is located in the old Town Hall, one block south of U.S. 2 on S. Main Street, 372-8792. Open 11–3 Monday–Saturday, May to September. Wheelchair accessible.

The **Iron River National Fish Hatchery** annually stocks 3.5 million lake trout into the Great Lakes. There is a small visitors center and you can walk around the giant inflatable domes where the fish are reared. Located seven miles north on Hwy A then one mile east on Fairview Road, 372-8510. Open 7–3:30 daily. Wheelchair accessible.

Catch a trophy-sized trout in one of the stocked, spring-fed **trout ponds** of the Iron River Trout Haus B&B. No fishing license needed, no limits, all equipment provided; they'll even clean and ice your catch. They also offer private **fly-fishing lessons** during some summer weekends. Located on the northwest edge of town at 205 Drummond Rd., 372-4219, 800/262-1453. Open 9–dusk Saturdays, Sundays, and holidays, weekdays by appointment. $

Kids can putt through 18 holes of fun at **TomKat Mini Golf**. Located on U.S. 2 on the east side of town, 372-8899. Open 12–10 daily, Memorial Day weekend to Labor Day. $

Moon Lake Park is a small but popular park with a picnic area, beach, playground, volleyball, boat launch, and campground with 29 electric sites and showers. Located a half mile south on Hwy H. Open May through October.

Options for horseback riding at **The Ranch** include short or long trail rides, picnic rides, and overnight trips. They also have hayrides. Located 17 miles east on Hwy H, 746-2490. Open daily by reservation weather permitting. $

Events

The **Blueberry Festival**, held during late July at Moon Lake Park, has canoe races, Blueberry Queen coronation, parade, carnival rides, live music, craft show, and how could a blueberry festival be complete without a pie-eating contest?

Shopping

You'll find a good selection at **Iron River Antiques**, 219 Mill St., 372-5257. Open Tuesday–Saturday, May through October.

Sunbonnet Turnabout is literally overflowing with antiques and collectibles, or as they like to call it, "sophisticated junque." Located at 704 Mill St., 372-8811. Open Monday–Saturday, May through October.

This Old Bunkhouse sells country-primitive crafts and some antiques in a quaint historic building. Located on U.S. 2 on the east end of town, 372-5599. Open Tuesday–Sunday, May through October.

The **White Winter Winery** specializes in mead (honey wine), but it also produces several fruit blends, such as strawberry, apple, blueberry, and raspberry. Ask for a tasting or tour. Besides wines it also sells wine- and beer-making supplies; Wisconsin food items like cheese, maple syrup, honey, and wild rice; and some high-quality gift items made by local artisans. Located at 402 S. George St., 372-5656. Open daily.

Sharing the same building is the **Java Trout Espresso/Internet Bar**, 372-5511, where you can get an espresso, cappuccino, Italian sodas, or any number of other drinks. Enjoy outdoor seating during the summer. Open daily.

Bicycling

The **Tri-County Corridor** (p. 79) passes through town and there is access to the **CAMBA trail system** (p. 42).

Where to Eat

The **Lumbermen's Restaurant and Lounge**, 421 Mill St., 372-8880, has pizza, broasted chicken, salads, sandwiches, steaks, seafood, and breakfast foods available all day. Open daily for breakfast, lunch, and dinner.

Besides the obvious, the **Pizza Parlor**, 407 S. Main St., 372-4005, also offers burgers and daily specials such as chicken or shrimp dinners. Open Tuesday–Sunday for dinner.

Rustic Roost, on U.S. 2 on the east end of town, 372-4426, is a basic family-style restaurant with sandwiches, steaks, seafood, and daily specials. Open daily except Wednesday for breakfast, lunch, and dinner.

Where to Stay

Bed-and-Breakfast

The **Iron River Trout Haus**, 205 Drummond Rd., 372-4219, 800/262-1453, sits on 40 wooded acres along the Iron River. The renovated rustic 1892 house has four guest rooms (two private baths, one shared) with themed decor. Enjoy the environmental library and art or the trout fishing (see p. 51). The regional gourmet breakfast includes fresh trout with a two-night stay.

Other Lodging

Best Western Lumbermen's Inn, 421 Mill St., 372-4515, 800/528-1234, has 31 rooms with cable TV.

The **Deer Trail Lodge**, 11 miles southeast on Hwy H, 372-8660, is a quiet guest-only facility on 30 acres overlooking Lake Delta surrounded by the Chequamegon National Forest (p. 48). The ten two-bedroom cottages have full kitchens and decks. Resort amenities include a beach, sauna, playground, common lodge, and a boat with each unit.

Delta Lodge, 12 miles south on Hwy H to Old Hwy H, 372-4299, sits on 70 acres bordering Lake Everett in the Chequamegon National Forest (p. 48). There are 12 well-spaced cottages, many with fireplaces and decks. Guests will enjoy the beach with a long dock and raft, playground and sporting facilities, lakeside nature trail, and boat provided with each unit. The historic main lodge has a restaurant/bar and game room.

Rustic Roost, at the east end of town on U.S. 2, 372-4426, has eight tiny log cabin cottages and six electric RV campsites.

South of town are two county-owned campgrounds. **Twin Bear Park**, 6.5 miles south on Hwy H, crams in 48 campsites with electricity. **Delta Lake Park**, 12 miles south on Hwy H to Old Hwy H, has 30 rustic campsites and is a much more peaceful setting. Both parks have a beach, picnic area, playground, and boat launch. Open May through October. For reservations call 372-8610.

Camping is also available at **Moon Lake Park** (p.51) and the **Chequamegon National Forest** (p. 48).

Emergencies

Call 373-6120. The nearest hospital is in Ashland.

More Information

Iron River Area Chamber, P.O. Box 448, Iron River 54847, 372-8558, www.iracc.com. Tourism information is available on U.S. 2 at the west edge of town.

Chapter 4
Garland City
Ashland, Bad River Reservation, Mellen, Glidden

Ashland

After you've been here a short while you'll understand why the people of Ashland call this "Lake Superior's Hometown." With nearly 8,800 residents Ashland, the county seat, is a large city by northern Wisconsin standards, but a thriving Main Street, beautiful parks, and an economy not entirely dependent on tourism give it an intimate, small-town feel.

The area's recorded history began in 1659 when French explorers Radisson and Groseilliers landed here and built a small cabin near an Ojibwe village: the first house built by any Europeans in what was to become Wisconsin. The area quickly became an important fur trade center and several tribes came here to do business with the French and later the British and Americans. Despite nearly 200 years of commerce in the area, the settlement that was to become Ashland wasn't founded until 1854 when Asaph Whittlesey and George Kilbourn rowed across Chequamegon Bay from La Pointe to form a city. They named it Whittlesey, but it became Ashland in 1860 when the town's postmaster decided to honor the Great Compromiser, Henry Clay, by using the name of Clay's Kentucky estate.

Settlers soon arrived with great expectations, but the nationwide financial panic of 1857, followed by the Civil War, dashed their hopes: eventually all but one family left. But by the 1870s Ashland was reborn when it was selected as the terminus of the Wisconsin Central Railroad, which reached town in 1877. Other railroads soon followed to transport the timber cut in one of the city's ten sawmills.

Ashland, blessed with an ideal natural harbor, became the area's primary port for shipping iron ore, lumber, and brownstone, which was quarried nearby. In addition, eastern coal was arriving to be transported to growing settlements in the West. Tourists also arrived in great numbers by rail or passenger steamer to stay in the fashionable Chequamegon and Knight Hotels.

This was Ashland's heyday and the city was known as the Garland City of the Inland Seas. Eventually the forests were cleared, the mines faded, and shipping moved west to Superior and Duluth, but the city has survived. The large number of fancy storefronts and Victorian mansions still here attest to the great amount of wealth that industry brought to this port city through the early part of this century.

Things to See and Do

For a good introduction to the region visit the new **Northern Great Lakes Center** which serves to educate visitors about this region through historical and ecological displays, multi-media presentation, special programs, area tourism information, and the State Historical Society of Wisconsin's regional archives. The land around the center attracts abundant wildlife (it has been proposed to become the Whittlesey Creek National Wildlife Refuge), and there are hiking trails and boardwalks to help you explore it. There is also a five-story observation tower and a gift shop. Located 2.5 miles west at the junction of U.S. 2 and Hwy 13, 685-9983. Open 8–6 daily. Wheelchair accessible.

The **Ashland Historical Society Museum**, housed in the 1869 Wilmarth Mansion, celebrates the city with historical displays and rooms filled with period fixtures. Interesting exhibits include antique dolls, hand-carved miniature circus wagons, and medical equipment. Don't miss the intricately carved woodworking on the fireplace. On Thursdays (and sometimes other days during the summer) you can watch people weave rugs on old-fashioned looms. The rugs are sold in the gift shop. The historical society also runs a genealogy and local history department. Located at 522 Chapple Ave., 682-4911. Open 10–2 Monday–Friday, plus Saturdays from May to September. $

Downtown Ashland retains an abundance of historic buildings. The **Ashland Main Street Historic District** (officially designated the West Second Street Historic District on the National Register of Historic Places) covers Main Street, between Sixth Avenue West and Ellis Avenue. Buildings of note include the old Ashland Post Office, which now serves as City Hall, at 601; Vaughn Library at 502; and Ashland County Courthouse at 201. Maps are available from the Chamber of Commerce.

Long abandoned, the historic **Soo Line Depot** is bustling once again after undergoing an award-winning, $1 million restoration in 1987. This 1889 brownstone building, listed on the National Register of Historic Places, now houses two restaurants, a microbrewery, offices, and what is claimed to be the world's largest collection of railroad art. An old steam locomotive is displayed out front. When built in 1900 it was the largest in the world and the only Decopad (10-wheel drive) ever built. Located at 400 Third Ave. W.

At the turn of the century the **Chapple Avenue** area, starting at Sixth Street and continuing south for several blocks, was Ashland's most elegant neighborhood. This is a great place to admire a variety of historic residences, including many beautifully restored mansions. **MacArthur Avenue**, one block west, also has many beautiful homes. The area has been proposed as an official historic district.

Ashland's lakefront has several parks with historic displays, picnic areas, and great lake views. **Bayview Park**, on the far east side of town, has an interesting replica frontier stockade, state historical marker about Fleet Admiral William D. Leahy, beach, a fishing pier at the remains of the Chicago and North Western ore dock, and Ashland's best lake views. At the end of the dock is **Tern Island**, where over half of all the endangered common terns in the Lake Superior region come from. Many other birds can be seen here too. This is the closest you can get to the **Ashland Breakwater Lighthouse** on land, but you'll still need binoculars to really appreciate it.

Kreher Park has a beach, playground, artesian well, boat launch, and 36 RV-only campsites with showers and dump station. The park sits at the foot of the impressive **Soo Line Ore Dock**, completed in 1925 and then the largest concrete structure of its kind (80 feet high, 59 feet wide, and 1800 feet long). It is the only remaining dock of five docks in Ashland that shipped iron ore from the mines of the Gogebic Range through the 1960s. Also here is **Just-4-Par Mini Golf**, open 11–10 daily during the summer, weekends in spring and fall.

Memorial Park is a small park with a large band shell. A historical marker next to several giant logs and a boat propeller discusses pulpwood rafting. There is also an old cannon.

Besides being the most popular swimming beach in Ashland, **Maslowski Beach**, on Ashland's far west side, has a small replica log cabin and state historical marker commemorating the Radisson-Groseilliers landing site. There is also a picnic area, artesian well, playground, and volleyball court.

Across the highway is 100-acre **Prentice Park** where you can observe abundant wildlife along the nature trails and boardwalks, enjoy the deer yard, or canoe through the adjacent state-owned **Fish Creek Sloughs**. There are also picnic areas, several artesian wells, a playground, and campground with 14 sites (nine electric).

Connecting several of the parks is the new **Waterfront Trail,** a paved multi-purpose path along the lakeshore still taking shape. It is the perfect spot for a leisurely stroll or a strenuous run or bike ride.

The **Ashland Agricultural Research Station** was created in 1906, near the end of the logging era, by the University of Wisconsin College of Agriculture to test new plant varieties and production methods for farming in the cutover land in northern Wisconsin, a mission it continues today. Self-guided tour sheets of the field crop demonstration areas are available at the office. It also offers gardening classes and agricultural field day demonstrations. Located 3.5 miles west on U.S. 2, 682-7268.

Events

Banjo-pickin', guitar-strummin', and flute-tooting musicians from across the nation have flocked to the **Northland Folk Festival** since 1972, making this the state's longest running folk festival. The two-day event, held in early May at Northland College, features both national performers and an open stage where everyone is welcome to perform. You can also attend workshops and buy various crafts. $

At the Bay Area Civic Center that same Saturday is **Scandinavian Heritage Day** with cultural displays; ethnic foods, music, and dancing; arts and crafts; and a genealogy booth.

Bay Days, a five-day event in mid-July, is Ashland's biggest celebration. The many events include bike, boat, and foot races; basketball tournament; a variety of kids' activities; arts and crafts fair; sidewalk sales; live music; fireworks; and the popular Mike Harvey Sock Hop.

The **Chequamegon Bay Rendezvous**, held in mid-August in Bayview Park, relives the fur trade era of the 1600s to 1650s with historic reenactments of the voyageurs and early settlers. $

The new **Whistlestop Festival**, held in mid-October, features a marathon, half-marathon, and relay; nonstop music ranging from polka to blues to gospel; and a classic car show. You also can enjoy a Lake Superior fish boil on Friday and sample microbrews on Saturday.

Shopping

There are three antique shops in Ashland. **Waterfront Antique & Gift Shoppe** also has a large selection of used books. Located at 1222 Lake Shore Dr. W, 682-9547. Open Tuesday–Saturday, April through October. **Northern Air Antiques**, a multi-dealer facility, also does custom airbrushing. Located at 516 W. Main St., 682-3339. Open daily.

The **Antique Inn** is located at 2016 Lake Shore Dr. E, 682-5452. Open Monday–Saturday.

Right next to the Antique Inn is **The Cheese House** where you can load up on such Wisconsin food products as cheese, maple syrup, jams and jellies, wild rice, and fudge, 682-5452. Open Monday–Saturday.

The **C.M.N. Doll Shop** creates handmade porcelain dolls that are sold throughout the Upper Midwest. It also sells clothes and other doll accessories, offers doll-making classes, and can do custom designs to your specifications. Located at 216 4th Ave. W, 682-9481. Open Wednesday, Thursday, and Saturday.

The **Chequamegon Food Co-op** sells natural and organic produce and other foods, plus bulk items and environmentally friendly products. Located at 215 Chapple Ave., 682-8251. Open Monday–Saturday.

The **New England Store**, in the restored 1884 Ashland National Bank, has high quality country-style crafts including a year-round Christmas selection. Located at 518 W. Main St., 682-2171. Open Monday–Saturday, plus Sundays from Memorial Day weekend to January.

Superior House has a fine selection of birdhouses, wind chimes, afghans, gourmet foods, children's gifts, and more. Located at 601 Lake Shore Dr. W, 682-7662. Open daily, May through October; Monday–Saturday, November and December; and most days the rest of the year.

The **Superior Water-Logged Lumber Gift Shoppe & Gallery** has a varied selection of artistic works and functional goods made by national and local artisans using its famous "Timeless Timber" (see p. 60). While this is high-quality stuff, much of it with accordingly high prices, some items are quite reasonable. There are no factory tours, but if you ask they might show you their million dollar, state-of-the-art "Big Daisy" sawmill. There is also a display room with a video. Located at 2200 Lake Shore Dr. E, 685-WOOD, 888/OLD-LOGS. Open Monday–Saturday.

Performing Arts

Northland College's **Alvord Theater** has many musical and theatrical performances during the school year. Call 682-1339 for information. $

There are regular summer concerts at the **Band Shell in Memorial Park**.

The **Chequamegon Theatre Association** (CTA) has produced community theater for over two decades. Located in the Rinehart

Timeless Timber

During the heyday of lumbering in the Northwoods many billions of board feet of lumber were floated on Lake Superior to mills in lakeside towns, and not all of it reached its destination. An estimated 10–20 percent of the logs sank into the lake's frigid depths where they remain to this day. Preserved by the cold water, the old-growth logs, some over 300 years old when cut, are in near-perfect condition despite having been submerged for a century or more.

Scott Mitchen frequently encountered these logs while scuba diving, but considered them a nuisance in his quest for shipwrecks. Eventually he took more of an interest after he made some inquiries and decided that this could be his biggest find ever. And he should know, because logs aren't the only valuables Mitchen has discovered over the years. He is, in fact, a noted treasure hunter, having recently found a seventeenth-century pirate ship, along with the cargo of 24,000 pounds of gold and silver. He founded the **Superior Water-Logged Lumber Company** in 1992, and since then Mitchen's innovative logging techniques have gained nationwide attention, including profiles by *USA Today, The Washington Post, The New York Times*, ABC and CBS News, CNN, and many others.

The logs are located with sonar and then either brought up with a crane or floated to the surface by attaching inflatable air bags. The company kiln-dries and cuts the logs, then sells every part possible, even the sawdust.

Though some appreciate the wood for the mystique, it isn't just the age that makes these logs special. By the very nature of having grown slowly in a mixed forest the grain is very fine and tight. One can expect 6–15 growth rings per inch in trees felled today. The Timeless Timber, Mitchen's trademarked name, has as many as 70 per inch. It also has a more figured grain prized by woodworkers. These differences have prompted artists from around the world to seek out the wood and have made them willing to pay as much as ten times the price of new wood.

Luthiers are among the most excited by the new venture. If the proper wood can be found some expect that violins made from these trees could rival those made by Antonio Stradivari some three hundred years ago. Analysis of the wood retrieved has shown similar characteristics to the wood used by the world's most famous violin maker.

Mitchen proudly calls this "environmentally friendly logging," since no new trees are felled, but not everyone is pleased with the recovery. Some are concerned that moving the logs will disturb historical sites and fish habitat or stir up polluted sediment. The U.S. Army Corps of Engineers and the Wisconsin Department of Natural Resources have approved the retrieval, but each area is first surveyed by the DNR and the State Historical Society. And, because the logs are legally considered unclaimed property, the State of Wisconsin receives a fee from the recovery and the money goes into the Common School Trust Fund.

Mitchen has estimated that there may be millions of logs on the bottom of Lake Superior. Some, including the DNR, doubt there are nearly that many, and recent recoveries by Mitchen and the few other companies that have followed (Superior Water-Logged Lumber remains the major player and the only company with its own sawmill) have been disappointing, but they place the blame on the slow permit process. Work still continues at full throttle in the mill, but many of the logs are purchased from other companies or recovered from other parts of the United States, Canada, and even Brazil. They have also applied for permits on inland lakes as well. No matter how many logs are recovered, many artisans are thrilled about the early lumber companies' bad luck.

Theatre at 210 E. Fifth Ave. (behind the Super Wash). Call 682-5554 for information. **$**

Golf

The nine-hole **Ashland Elks Golf Course**, half a mile west on Hwy 137, 682-8004, has good views of Lake Superior.

Marinas/Charters

The **Port of Ashland Marina & Yacht Club** at the end of Ellis Avenue, 682-7049, is a full service marina with 110 slips for seasonal and transient dockage.

Anglers All specializes in fly fishing and light tackle in Chequamegon Bay and inland waters and can also arrange Lake Superior charters. Casting instruction is available. Located at 2803 Lake Shore Dr. E, 682-5754.

Lou Bickel of **Lou's Charter Service** offers Lake Superior fishing trips. Call 682-2646 or ask around at the marina.

Bicycling

You can bike on the **Waterfront Trail** (p. 58) and the **Tri-County Corridor** (p. 79), which ends in Prentice Park (p.57).

Outdoor Rentals

Bodin's, on U.S. 2/Hwy 13 on the far west side of town, 682-6441, rents bikes, cross-country skis, and snowshoes.

Spectator Sports

A.B.C. Raceway has Saturday night stock car races from May through August and hosts the Red Clay Classic, a WISSOTA-sanctioned invitational stock car race, in late September or early October. Located 2.5 miles south on Hwy 13 then one mile west on Butterworth Road, 682-4990. **$**

The cars head to Chequamegon Bay for **ice racing** every Sunday from mid-January to mid-March.

Where to Eat

The **Black Cat Coffee House**, 211 Chapple Ave., 682-3680, is the hippest place in Ashland—and has some of the best food. Besides filling all your caffeinated needs the diverse menu, using many locally grown organic ingredients, is constantly evolving: look for pasta, pizza, and Mexican dishes. Deli sandwiches, soups, salads, and fresh bakery are also always available. It has outdoor seating and live music on most weekends. Open daily for breakfast, lunch, and dinner.

The old Soo Line Depot (p. 56), 400 Third Ave. W, with its elegant decor, houses two of the Northland's finest restaurants. Both are open daily for lunch and dinner. The top-quality meals at **The Depot**, 682-4200, include steaks, fresh seafood, pasta primavera, seasonal specialties, and the signature dish: prime rib of beef au jus. They use many locally grown organic vegetables and herbs.

In the same building **The Railyard Pub**, 682-9199, has a more informal atmosphere and a creative menu. Try one of the unique sandwiches and entrees such as BBQ ostrich burger, Southwestern buffalo burger, black bean veggie burger, or chicken jambalaya. There are also soups, salads, and a kid's menu. Both restaurants serve a variety of microbrews from the **South Shore Brewery**, also located in the building. The copper brewing vessels are visible in The Railyard. You can take home bottles of your favorite brews.

Golden Glow Cafe and Ice Cream Parlour, 519 W. Main St., 682-2838, has a large menu of basic family fare plus Mexican food on Tuesdays, but order your meal with dessert in mind. Open daily for breakfast (free coffee) and lunch, and weekdays for dinner.

Besides the obvious, **Hugo's Pizza**, 221 Sanborn Ave., 682-8202, also has sandwiches, lasagna, chicken, salad bar, and a Friday fish fry. Open Monday–Friday for lunch and dinner and Saturday and Sunday for dinner. Delivery is available.

The Marine Club, one mile west on U.S. 2/Hwy 13, 682-3298, has an extensive seafood menu plus steaks, salads, and daily specials. The dining room overlooks the bay. Open daily for dinner.

The **New China Restaurant**, 300 Lake Shore Dr. W, 682-6601, has been serving Chinese favorites for over 20 years. It has a large and varied menu with many lunch specials. Open daily for lunch and dinner.

Even if you're not staying there, you can still enjoy the ambiance of the Hotel Chequamegon at **Sirtoli's Italian Steak House and Molly Cooper's Lounge**, 101 Lake Shore Dr. W, 682-9095, 800/946-5555. The menu includes steaks, seafood, pastas, and daily specials. If you're lucky you'll be able to get a seat on the deck overlooking the bay. Open daily for breakfast, lunch, and dinner.

Where to Stay

Bed-and-Breakfast

The **Residenz**, 723 Chapple Ave., 682-2425, is in the heart of the historic Chapple Avenue neighborhood. The 1889 Queen Anne Victorian home, built by Clarence Lamoreux, a state senator and prominent attorney, is filled with period decor. Each of the three guest rooms has a private attached bath. A full breakfast is served in the formal dining room.

Other Lodging

All hotels and motels in Ashland are along Lake Shore Drive (though the address may not show it) and in sight of Lake Superior. The closer the address is to zero, the nearer it is to downtown.

AmericInn Motel, 3009 Lake Shore Dr. E, 682-9950, 800/634-3444, has 49 rooms, including some Jacuzzi suites, with cable TV, indoor pool, whirlpool, and sauna.

Anderson's Chequamegon Motel, 2200 Lake Shore Dr. W, 682-4658, 800/727-2776, has 18 rooms with cable TV. Some waterbeds are available.

Ashland Motel, 2300 Lake Shore Dr. W, 682-5503, has 43 rooms with cable TV.

Bayview Motel, 2419 Lake Shore Dr. E, 682-5253, 800/249-3200, has eight rooms with cable TV.

Best Western Holiday House, one mile west on U.S. 2/Hwy 13, 682-5235, 800/528-1234, has 65 rooms with cable TV, indoor pool, whirlpool, and sauna.

Crest Motel, west side of town on Lake Shore Dr. W, 682-6603, has 24 rooms with cable TV.

Harbor Motel, 1206 Lake Shore Dr. W, 682-5211, has 17 rooms with cable TV.

Hotel Chequamegon, 101 Lake Shore Dr. W, 682-9095, 800/946-5555, is modeled after the landmark Chequamegon Hotel built in 1877 and destroyed by fire 80 years later. The original hotel was the pinnacle of sophistication in Ashland and the new hotel follows in its path. The 64 rooms with cable TV range from singles to deluxe Jacuzzi suites. Guests can enjoy an indoor pool, whirlpool, and sauna.

Lake Aire Inn, 104 N. Ellis Ave., 682-4551, 888/666-2088, has 25 rooms with cable TV, whirlpool, sauna, game room, exercise room, and free continental breakfast.

Lakeside Motel, 1706 Lake Shore Dr. W, 682-4575, has 10 rooms with cable TV.

Super 8 Motel, 1610 Lake Shore Dr. W, 682-9377, 800/800-8000, has 70 rooms with cable TV, indoor pool, whirlpool, sauna, and free continental breakfast.

Town Motel, 920 Lake Shore Dr. W, 682-5555, has 12 rooms with cable TV.

Camping is available at **Kreher Park** (p. 57) and **Prentice Park** (p. 57).

Emergencies

Call 911. Memorial Medical Center, 1615 Maple Ln., 682-4563.

More Information

Ashland Area Chamber of Commerce, P.O. Box 746, Ashland 54806, 682-2500, 800/284-9484, www.ashlandchamber.org. The chamber offices are at the Bay Area Civic Center, 340 Fourth Ave. W.

Camping in Chequamegon National Forest

A Call 264-2511, **B** Call 739-6334. These also have first-come, first-served sites.

The campgrounds are officially open May through October. Winter camping is allowed, but facilities are not maintained and only Day Lake is plowed.

Bad River Reservation

The largest of the six Ojibwe reservations in Wisconsin, the Bad River Reservation covers 56,283 acres, with 17 miles of Lake Superior shoreline, almost all of which remain wild.

Odanah (pronounced o-day-nuh) is the reservation's only settlement, though the area around the casino is now known as New Odanah. This widely scattered community is home to most of the roughly 1,000 people who live on the reservation. Odanah, which is the Ojibwe word for village, was founded in 1845 at a site known as Old Indian Gardens because the Ojibwe had long planted gardens here. During the logging boom around the turn of the century when a sawmill was located here this was a bustling town of well over 2,000 people.

At the reservation's northern tip is the Kakagon and Bad River Sloughs (sounds like "news"), a National Natural Landmark often called Wisconsin's Everglades. The 16,000 acres of marsh and backwater channels is teeming with wildlife: it is especially important for spawning fish and migrating birds. The sloughs hold a special significance to the Ojibwe who harvest the plentiful wild rice each fall.

Things to See and Do

Bad River Casino, on U.S. 2 in Odanah, 682-7768, 800/777-7449, has blackjack, video poker and keno, pull-tabs, and hundreds of slot machines. There is frequent live entertainment and special events. The casino also has a smoke shop. You must be 21 or older to enter the casino. Open daily. Wheelchair accessible.

Bad River Bingo has a game at 1 p.m. Sunday in the Community Center. Located 0.75 mile west of the casino on U.S. 2 then just north on Maple Street. Call the casino for information.

The **Bad River Fish Hatchery** has released over 21 million walleye into the Bad River system. There are no visitor facilities, but you're welcome to have a look during April and May before the fish are released. Located on the west side of the reservation at the end of Indian Route 52, which joins U.S. 2 near the historical marker.

You can get a cursory look at the **Kakagon and Bad River Sloughs** from the fish hatchery or from Goslin Road, off U.S. 2 on the west side of the reservation, but to really see them you need to get out on the water. You can launch a canoe onto the Bad River at the U.S. 2 bridge and you can access the Kakagon River at the hatchery. The entire Bad River through the reservation is a good paddling destination.

Waverly Beach, some of the most beautiful sand beach along Lake Superior's south shore, is found on the east side of the reservation. Besides swimming you can hike for miles in either direction. Located 0.75 mile east of the casino on U.S. 2 then 3.5 miles northeast on Lake Road.

Even more remote, and just as beautiful, is **Bad River Falls**, a very long and wide series of ledges on the Bad River. Wildlife abounds here (when I visited two bald eagles flew overhead and animal tracks far outnumbered human ones on the trail), and the half-mile or so path leading to the falls is itself a worthy destination. The unmarked but easy to follow trail splits at the start though both branches lead to the same spot. When the trail hits the river head south to the falls. Located 0.25 mile west of the casino on U.S. 2, 0.5 mile west on Miller Road, eight miles south on Pine Flat Road, and 2.75 miles west on Falls Road.

Events

The **Manomin Powwow**, held the third weekend in August, celebrates the annual wild rice harvest with native dancing and music. **$**

Shopping

You'll be drawn in to **Airguns, Cameras & Collectibles** by the antiques displayed outside, and inside you will find quality used items, which include . . . airguns, cameras, and collectibles. Located on U.S. 2 at the far west side of the reservation, you can't miss it, 682-9132. Open daily, "unless I'm somewhere else."

If you stop at the **Three Eagles Gift & Smoke Shop** for gas, tobacco, or alcohol you'll be surprised by the selection, and quality, of Native American jewelry and art. Located 2.5 miles east of Ashland on U.S. 2, 682-8844. Open daily.

Where to Eat

You have three dining options, all at the casino. There is a **snack shop** in the gambling hall offering drinks or a quick bite to eat. For sit-down meals there is **Dream Catcher's**, in a log cabin adjoining the casino, offering basic family-style meals plus a salad bar, Friday fish fry, and Saturday prime rib. Or you could try the new all-you-can-eat **Bad River Buffet**, which has a different theme every day, such as Italian, Mexican, seafood, or home cooking. All three are open daily for breakfast, lunch, and dinner.

Where to Stay

The **Bad River Lodge**, adjoining the casino, 682-6102, 800/795-7121, has 50 rooms including some Jacuzzi suites, with indoor pool, whirlpool, game room, and free continental breakfast. Serious gamblers will want to take advantage of the "stay and play" benefits.

Emergencies

Call 911. The nearest hospital is in Ashland.

More Information

Bad River Band of Lake Superior Chippewa, P.O. Box 39, Odanah 54861, 682-7111.

Mellen

Mellen, a quiet town of 961 people, sits along the Bad River at the edge of the Penokee-Gogebic Range. Iron City, as it was originally known, was founded in 1896 along the busy rail line between Ashland and Chicago. But it was the branch line running east, built to transport the iron ore from the legendary mines of Wisconsin and Upper Michigan, that helped the town to thrive. Logging and tanning were also important early enterprises, and the wood products industry remains vital to the economy today, as is evident by the large plants around town.

The city's train depot was named for Charles Mellen, a railroad official, and the town later acquired this name since the conductor called out the station name instead of Iron City upon arrival.

Things to See and Do

Picturesque **Mellen City Hall** is listed on the National Register of Historic Places. The 1896 Victorian building houses city government offices, the police and fire departments, and the library. On the second floor is the **Mellen Area Museum**, a small collection of local historical memorabilia. Located at the corner of Main Street and Bennett Avenue, 274-8331. Open when volunteers are available; no regular hours; inquire in the library.

Copper Falls State Park is one of the most popular state parks in northern Wisconsin and with good reason. It has several beautiful waterfalls and a narrow, rugged gorge surrounding the Bad River with walls up to 100 feet high. The namesake falls is just 12 feet tall, though Brownstone Falls at 40 feet is Wisconsin's seventh highest waterfall. There are wheelchair-accessible overlooks. While many people come to just see the waterfalls and the gorge, there is a lot more to do in this nearly 2,700-acre park. There are nine miles of hiking trails, 4.25 miles of challenging off-road bike trails, and 14 miles of groomed cross-country ski trails. There are also a swimming beach and canoe landing on Loon Lake, summer nature programs, picnic areas, ball field, and playground. Lake Superior and the Apostle Islands are visible from atop the observation tower. There are 55 campsites (13 electric, wheelchair-accessible sites) with showers, dump station, and two secluded backpacking sites along the Bad River. The park is located two miles north on Hwy 169, 274-5123. Open year-round. **$**

An eight-mile stretch of the **North Country National Scenic Trail** (p. 98) winds through Copper Falls State Park and continues on to Mellen. Another section of the North Country Trail begins 2.5 miles west on FR 390 (Hillcrest Drive) and continues for 61 miles through the **Chequamegon National Forest** (p.48).

Also in the Chequamegon are two superb vistas. The **Penokee Overlook**, just a short, easy walk up a set of steps to the wonderful views of the Penokee-Gogebic range to the south and east. There are informational markers here too. This is also the trailhead for the 7.6-mile **Penokee Mountain Trail** which shares part of its path with the North Country Trail. The three loops are groomed for cross-country skiing. Located three miles west on Hwy GG. $

The trail leading to **Morgan Falls and St. Peter's Dome** is a beautiful hike with spectacular destinations. Morgan Falls, an easy 0.6 miles from the trailhead, makes a narrow 70-foot drop down several steps. It is the second highest waterfall in the state. The 1.8-mile hike to the top of St. Peter's Dome takes a lot more effort, but the views from the highest point in the forest (1,600 feet above sea level) make it worthwhile. The Apostle Islands are visible on clear days. The trailhead is located 8.5 miles west on Hwy GG, 4.5 miles northwest on FR 187, and five miles northwest on FR 199. $

Big Spruce Stable offers private guided trail rides through the wooded Penokee foothills plus Western riding lessons and individual buggy rides for those who would rather not ride horseback. Located two miles north on Hwy 13 then 0.75 mile west on Hwy C, 274-2522. Open daily Memorial Day weekend to Labor Day and weekends (and maybe some weekdays, but you'll need to call to find out) weather permitting the rest of the year. $

If you'd like to try **dog sledding** call George Tresnak at 274-2401. He offers day trips or overnight treks in the Chequamegon National Forest (p. 48). $

Golf

The **Mellen Country Club**, two miles north on Hwy 13 then 0.5 mile west on Hwy C, 274-7311, has a 9-hole course.

Bicycling

There are mountain bike trails in **Copper Falls State Park** (p. 68), plus you can ride on the **North Country National Scenic Trail** (p. 98) between town and the park as well as in the **Chequamegon National Forest** (p. 48).

The **Penokee Range Bike Race** is a 47-mile, WISPORT-sanctioned ride through the Chequamegon National Forest held in August. The less competitive can join a tour.

Where to Eat

The Steak Out, 129 E. Bennett Ave., 274-2171, serves basic family fare including steaks and sandwiches. The Friday fish fry goes beyond the basics offering several choices, such as salmon, walleye, and catfish. Saturday brings prime rib. Open Tuesday–Sunday for breakfast, lunch, and dinner.

Where to Stay

Mellen Motel, 0.75 mile south on Hwy 13/77, 274-2301, has five rooms with cable TV.

Camping is available at **Copper Falls State Park** (p.68) and the **Chequamegon National Forest** (p. 48).

Emergencies

Call 800/472-6927. The nearest hospital is in Ashland.

More Information

Mellen Area Chamber of Commerce, P.O. Box 793, Mellen 54546, 274-2330. In town the chamber offices are at 125 E. Bennett Ave.

Glidden

This is the "Black Bear Capital of Wisconsin," as the people of Glidden go out of their way to remind you: black bear banners decorate the streets, and bears figure into the names of many area businesses.

Initially called Chippewa Crossing, the town lies near the headwaters of the East Fork Chippewa River, which passes through town. Each spring during the logging boom, timber from surrounding logging camps was floated from here to sawmills downstream. The name was changed to Glidden in the 1870s when the railroad reached town to honor of one of the rail company's executives.

Things to See and Do

Cementing its claim as Black Bear Capital, Glidden is the final resting place of the **world's largest black bear**. The enormous animal, 7 feet 10 inches and 665 pounds, was shot five miles northeast of town in 1963. It took seven men to haul it out of the woods. The bear is now on permanent display in a small building two blocks east of Hwy 13 on Grant Street.

Displayed alongside the bear is, according to the signs, the **"world's largest white pine log"** and **"biggest and last sleigh-hauled log**, Dec 21, 1984." The thick section of lumber, still on the sleds, is impressive, despite the dubious claims.

Marion Park has a picnic area, playground, ball field, horseshoe pits, and an army tank on display, but most tourists stop here to see the dome-topped **Marion Park Pavilion**, listed on the National Register of Historic Places. When it was built in 1938 the octagonal building was the state's largest self-supported domed structure. Looking inside at the large hardwood floor, surrounded by a ring of windows, you can easily picture an old-fashioned barn dance. Many community events are held here.

Also in the park is the **Glidden Area Historical Society Museum** with a variety of items housed in two bare-bones buildings. Basically if it's old, they'll put it in here. Located 0.75 miles west of Hwy 13 on W. Park Street, 264-6004. Open only during special events, though in the future they hope to line up enough volunteers to open summer weekends. Wheelchair accessible.

The **Chequamegon National Forest Glidden Ranger Station** is the place to go for information about the nearby forest's (p. 48) numerous recreational opportunities. There are also animal displays and a small gift shop. Located 0.75 miles north on Hwy 13, 264-2511 voice/TTY. Open 7:30–4 weekdays and 7:15–3:45 weekends.

The forest has three main attractions in this area. The **Day Lake Recreation Area** has a picnic area, campground, beach, wheelchair-accessible viewing platform/fishing pier, and boat launch. There is also an easy mile-long interpretive trail along the shore of Day Lake. The 640-acre lake has many islands and floating bogs and is a noted spot for watching wildlife. Located three miles northwest on Hwy 13, 14 miles west on Hwy 77, and 0.5 mile west on Hwy M. $

The **Dead Horse Run Trail** is a 48-mile system developed for ATV and motorcycle riders though it is also open to nonmotorized travel if you so desire. The easiest access is three miles northwest on Hwy 13 then 11 miles west on Hwy 77.

The 6.5-mile **West Torch River Trail** is a series of gently rolling loops especially popular with cross-country skiers. Also here is the **Beautiful Pine Walk**, a 0.25-mile interpretive nature trail. Located three miles northwest on Hwy 13, 13.5 miles west on Hwy 77, and 2.5 miles south on Hwy GG. $

The **East Fork Chippewa River** in Mellen is a good canoe route. The river eventually passes through the Chequamegon National Forest (p. 48) before it reaches the Chippewa Flowage (p. 109).

The **Great Divide Wayside**, 5.75 miles north along Hwy 13/77, is just your typical roadside rest stop, except for its location. This spot marks the northern continental divide. All rain falling north of this point ends up in Lake Superior; to the south the water finds its way to the Mississippi River.

Elk

Elk are roaming Wisconsin's forests once again. The last time that happened was in the mid-1800s. In May of 1995 the U.S. Forest Service, DNR, and University of Wisconsin–Stevens Point joined forces to reintroduce the lost ungulate to Wisconsin. Twenty-five elk were released in the Chequamegon National Forest south of Clam Lake to study the possibility of a permanent return. The program has been a resounding success with the herd nearly doubling after the first three years, and it's almost certain that bugling will once again be a permanent part of autumn in the Northwoods.

Scenic Drive

The **Great Divide National Forest Scenic Byway** traverses the heart of the Chequamegon National Forest (p. 48) roughly following the northern continental divide which separates the watersheds of the Great Lakes and the Mississippi River—though it does so more in spirit than geography since the actual divide is many miles to the north. The marked route begins north of Glidden and follows Hwy 77 for 29 miles west to Lost Land Lake in Sawyer County. A brochure about the route is available from the forest headquarters (p. 71).

Events

The **Glidden Community Fair**, held Labor Day weekend in Marion Park, features carnival rides, arts and crafts, frog-jumping contest, wacky Olympics, bingo, horse pull, mud run, and live music.

Where to Eat

Glidden Black Bear Bakery & Pizza, 246 Grant St., 264-2407, has sandwiches, ice cream, frozen yogurt, plus fresh bakery and pizza, of course. Take-out only. Open Tuesday–Friday for breakfast, lunch, and dinner and Saturdays for breakfast and lunch.

Kountry Korners, downtown on Hwy 13, 264-2066, offers no-frills home cooking featuring sandwiches, chicken, and daily lunch specials. Open Monday–Saturday for breakfast and lunch and Sunday for breakfast.

Where to Stay

Schroeder's Motel, two blocks east of Hwy 13 on Grant Street, 264-4401, has six basic rooms with cable TV.

Camping is available in the **Chequamegon National Forest** (p. 48).

Emergencies

Call 800/472-6927. The nearest hospital is Flambeau Hospital, 98 Sherry Ave., Park Falls, 762-2484.

More Information

Glidden Chamber of Commerce, P.O. Box 265, Glidden 54527, 264-4304.

Chapter 5
Twin Ports
Superior, Duluth

Superior

Northwest Wisconsin's largest city lives in the shadow of Duluth, Minnesota, its larger and more glamorous neighbor across the bay. Superior, a working-class town full of hometown pride, is sometimes—unjustifiably—overlooked by visitors to the region. The city of 27,455 is a little rough around the edges, but there is more than enough to see and do here to warrant a visit.

French voyageurs, who began arriving in the mid-seventeenth century, called this area Fond du Lac (head of the lake) and like the Native Americans before them camped in the natural harbor for protection from Lake Superior's notorious sudden storms. The first French settlement came in 1679 when Daniel Greysolon, Sieur du Lhut, for whom Duluth is named, arrived to promote peace between the warring Ojibwe and Sioux (not out of humanitarian concern, but to increase fur trade profits). He established a fur trading post on the Minnesota side of the St. Louis River and was later followed by many traders.

Permanent settlers began arriving here in 1853 in response to excitement over the soon-to-open Sault Sainte Marie Locks, and the next year a military road was completed between St. Paul and Superior bringing hundreds more people to Superior. As a site for a city, the head of the lakes couldn't be more ideal. The natural harbor is one of the best in the world—large and completely protected from storms—and as the furthest point west on the Great Lakes it is ideal from a commercial standpoint. The south side of the bay, where Superior was established, was the logical location for a city for many reasons: it had level terrain, as opposed to the steep hills of Duluth; was closest to the natural harbor entry; and rail connections to other cities wouldn't need to cross the St. Louis River. All indications were that Superior would not just be larger than its neighbor, but might rival Chicago in size and importance.

Wealthy land speculators from St. Paul and Washington politicians including Stephen A. Douglas, the famous debate partner of Abraham Lincoln (for whom Douglas County is named), actively promoted Superior, and by 1857 it had about 3,000 inhabitants, while Duluth remained a tiny village. Several plans were promoted to bring a railroad to the growing city, but that year's nationwide financial panic, followed by the Civil War, put these plans on hold and caused most of its citizens to abandon the young city.

It would be over two decades before anyone again dreamed of a great city at the head of the lakes; that person was eastern financier Jay Cooke, who came to a rundown Superior in 1868. The first railroad was planned for Superior but instead went to Duluth in 1870. It was to be the first in a series of events that would eventually make Duluth the dominant city and spark an intense rivalry between the two cities that to a small degree still exists today. At that time neighbors across the bay referred to each other as either "cliff dwellers" or "swamp jumpers."

Superior finally got its rail line in 1881, and soon area logging, mining, and Western wheat farming brought prosperity to both cities fueling construction of even more wharves, docks, and grain elevators to ship these products east. Shipping wasn't the only industry that flourished in Superior: fishing, woodworking, manufacturing, flour milling, and ship building all benefited from the easy access to the area's raw materials. Though eclipsed by Duluth, Superior was still Wisconsin's second largest city at the turn of the century.

The Twin Ports soon became the busiest port on the Great Lakes, a title it maintains today, shipping around 40 million tons of cargo annually. The grain elevators, ore docks, and shipyards—some of the largest in the world—dominate the shoreline, and ship watching is a popular pastime with locals and tourists alike.

Things to See and Do

The center of summer recreation in Superior is **Barker's Island**, a manmade island in Superior Bay that is home to some of the city's main attractions. Barker's has the city's marina, fishing and sailing charters, a hotel, plus summer concerts and other special events. You'll also enjoy a beach, picnic areas, playground, wheelchair-accessible fishing pier, and **Capt'n J's Miniature Golf**, a kid friendly 18-hole course. The island is reached from E. Second Street at Belknap Street, across from the Tourist Information Center.

The highlight of the island is the one-of-a-kind **S.S. Meteor Whaleback Ship and Maritime Museum**. Launched in 1896 the *Meteor* is the only remaining whaleback ship and is listed on the National Register of Historic Places. The whalebacks, with their unique rounded hulls, led to the improved designs used in today's massive freighters. Guided tours take you from the pilothouse to the boiler room. The museum in the ship's cargo hold has a collection of shipping memorabilia. Every October around Halloween it becomes a haunted ship with costumed ghosts and ghouls lurking around every corner. There are toned-down daytime versions for young children. 392-5742. Open 10–5 daily, mid-May through Labor Day, and weekends through early October. $

Next to the *Meteor* is the **Col. D.D. Gaillard**, the last of the U.S. Corps of Engineers steam-powered dredges and the largest of its kind. It handled the most difficult sections of the St. Lawrence Seaway between 1916 and 1982. It's a bit run down, but interesting.

The 10-foot bronze **Seaman's Memorial Statue**, erected shortly after the sinking of the *Edmund Fitzgerald*, honors all seamen who lost their lives on Lake Superior.

Get the full scoop on Twin Ports shipping by taking a ride with **Vista Fleet Harbor Tours**. The 1.75-hour narrated tours take you through the harbor for up-close views of the giant ships, grain elevators, and ore docks plus you'll pass under Duluth's famous Aerial Lift Bridge (p. 86). There are also lunch, dinner, and moonlight cruises. The fully enclosed boats depart from Barker's Island as well as from Duluth, 394-6846, 218/722-6218. Tours run daily from mid-May to mid-September and weekends through mid-October. Wheelchair accessible. $

Overlooking Barker's Island is the **Fairlawn Mansion and Museum**, a striking 42-room Victorian mansion built in 1890 by Martin Pattison, a timber and mining tycoon and Superior's second mayor. The house, listed on the National Register of Historic Places, has a beautiful interior adorned with marble and intricate woodwork and fully furnished with turn-of-the-century furnishings. The second and third floors also house the small collection of the Douglas County Historical Society, which includes displays on transportation, weaving, and many interesting old photos. Fairlawn hosts many special events such as concerts and lectures and has a small gift shop. Located at 906 E. Second St., 394-5712. Open daily, guided tours at 9, 11, 1, and 3. First floor is wheelchair accessible. $

Twin Ports Ship Watching

Between mid-March and mid-January foreign vessels' "salties" from around the globe and huge "lakers" which can stretch over 1,000 feet in length come to the Twin Ports to load and unload their cargo. Assuming you're not here in the dead of winter there are two ways to guarantee seeing a working ship in the harbor: take the **Vista Fleet Harbor Tours** (p. 76) or call the 24-hour **Boat Watcher's Hotline** (218/722-6489). The latter is a service of the U.S. Army Corps of Engineers that details area ship traffic.

You can see ships all across the Twin Ports, but the following are choice viewing spots. On most days several ships pass under the **Aerial Lift Bridge,** (p. 86) which is the single best place in the Twin Ports to see them. They pass so close you feel as if you can reach out and touch them. The **Lake Superior Maritime Visitor Center** (p. 86) has computer screens posting ship arrival and departure times. (These are just estimates, however, so you should ask upstairs at the information desk.) You should also pick up **"Great Lakes Shipping: A Guide,"** a free informative brochure published by the U.S. Army Corps of Engineers that will help you identify the various ships.

The **Duluth, Missabe, and Iron Range Railway Company observation platform** allows up-close viewing of ship loading at its ore docks, which extend over 2,000 feet into the harbor. From S. Fortieth Ave. W, just south of I-35, head east on Oneota Street and follow the signs.

In Superior your best bet is to drive past the docks on **Connors Point,** located one mile northwest of the Tourist Information Center on U.S. 53. There is a small, seldom-used picnic area at the end.

You should also try the **Harvest States grain elevators,** the largest in the U.S., along N. First Street. From the parking area under the Blatnik Bridge you can get right next to any ships in the eastern dock, assuming it's not blocked by waiting trucks.

There is less traffic here than at the Duluth Ship Canal by the Aerial Lift Bridge, but ships do arrive and depart through the **Superior Entry** at the end of Wisconsin Point (p. 79). These are announced on the Boat Watcher's Hotline.

The **Old Firehouse and Police Museum** is housed in an 1898 brick firehouse in the neighborhood that was Superior's first downtown. Firefighting equipment makes up the majority of the items on display; highlights include a 1906 horse-drawn steam pumper and a 1944 fire engine. The museum has also been designated Wisconsin's Police and Fire Hall of Fame. Located at 402 Twenty-third Ave. E, 398-7558. Open 10–5 daily from June through August. Partially wheelchair accessible. $

The small **Kruk Art Gallery** on the University of Wisconsin–Superior campus displays works by faculty, students, and guest artists. It may not be the Louvre, but a recent exhibition did include works by Picasso and Warhol. You'll usually find additional work one floor up in the **Third Floor Gallery**. Located in the Holden Fine and Applied Arts Center at the corner of Catlin Avenue and Nineteenth Street, 394-8391. Open weekdays during the school year, call for times. Wheelchair accessible.

The **Burlington Northern Ore Docks** are among the largest in the world. These monstrous docks have handled well over a billion tons of iron ore. There is an observation platform next to a state historical marker located one block east of E. Second St. on Thirty-seventh Avenue E then north to the end of E. First Street, but you'll get better views by walking down a short ways to the Osaugie Trail or from the end of Wisconsin Point (p. 79).

The **Davidson Windmill**, listed on the National Register of Historic Places, is one of the more unique sites in the state. The eight-bladed Finnish-style mill (unlike Dutch models with four) was built in 1904 by Finnish immigrant Jacob Davidson. It hasn't ground any wheat since 1926, but his descendants have worked to maintain it. Located 6.5 miles southeast of Superior on Hwy 13, near the Amnicon River.

The small village of Poplar, 13 miles east of Superior, is the hometown of Richard Bong, who earned the title "America's Ace of Aces" by downing a record 40 enemy planes during World War II. One block north of U.S. 2 on Memorial Drive is the **Richard I. Bong Memorial** with displays about his life and accomplishments. Open 9–5 daily from Memorial Day weekend to Labor Day and 9–3:30 (often earlier and later) weekdays during the school year, but if you come at another time and really want to see it stop by the hardware store and ask if anyone can open it up for you. Wheelchair accessible. A state historical marker about Major Bong is situated along U.S. 2.

A greatly expanded **Richard I. Bong Heritage Center** honoring all the men and women who served during World War II, on both the war and home front, is planned for Superior. It is expected to open in the next few years on U.S. 2/53 at the entrance to Barker's Island. It will house a restored Lockheed P-38 Lightning, the plane flown by Major Bong in the Pacific theater, plus historical displays, films, and interactive exhibits about WWII.

> ## Tri-County Corridor
>
> The Tri-County Corridor parallels U.S. 2 for 62 miles between Ashland's Prentice Park (p. 57) and Superior where it joins the Osaugie Trail (p. 82). The trail, one lane of which is surfaced with crushed limestone for bicyclists, is also open to horses, ATVs, motorcycles, and snowmobiles. For more information contact any of the area chambers or call 800/472-6338.

Wisconsin Point is an ideal place to swim, picnic, or just stroll along Lake Superior. The beautiful, wooded three-mile peninsula features an undisturbed beach full of agates and driftwood. Birdwatchers flock here during the spring and fall migration. There is a seventeenth-century Ojibwe burial site where people still leave objects in remembrance. At the end of the road you can see the Wisconsin Point Lighthouse and occasionally watch ships passing through the only natural entry to the harbor (see p. 77). Follow U.S. 2/53 to the south edge of town and head east for 1.5 miles on Moccasin Mike Road.

The **Superior Municipal Forest**, the largest municipal forest in the United States and one of the region's most popular cross-country skiing destinations, covers 4,500 acres. The 28 kilometers of trails are groomed for traditional and skate skiing in the winter and can be used year-round for hiking or mountain biking. The main trailhead is located on Twenty-eighth Street at Wyoming Avenue. The most scenic trail leads out along a narrow peninsula through the Dwight's Point and Pokegama Wetlands State Natural Area. It can be accessed from Billings Drive, 2.5 miles south of Twenty-eighth Street. The narrow bays make good paddling destinations and you can launch a canoe at several spots along Billings Drive. A walk-through archery course is located at Billings Drive and Forty-second Street. $ for cross-country skiing.

While all of **Pattison State Park**'s 1,400 acres are beautiful, the park's two waterfalls draw most visitors. Big Manitou Falls, the highest waterfall in Wisconsin and fourth highest east of the Rockies, drops 165 feet; just upstream is 31-foot Little Manitou Falls, the state's eighth highest. Big Manitou has wheelchair-accessible overlooks. Big Manitou Falls, a sacred spot to the Ojibwe and one of the most beautiful sights in the state, was almost destroyed by a dam planned for the Black River. Thankfully, Martin Pattison, a wealthy Superior businessman (see Fairlawn Mansion, p. 76), secretly purchased the land around the falls and donated it to the state for use as a park. After seeing the falls, hike the nearly eight miles of trails, paddle around or swim in 27-acre Interfalls Lake, visit the nature center, or join one of the many summer nature programs. Cross-country skiing is popular in the winter. There are 59 campsites (18 with electrical hookups, wheelchair-accessible site), showers, dump station, plus three isolated but easy-to-reach backpacking sites. The park is located 12 miles south of Superior on Hwy 35, 399-3111. $

At **Amnicon Falls State Park** the Amnicon River drops over not one but three roughly 20-foot waterfalls in a turbulent 100-yard stretch. A smaller fourth waterfall runs during high water levels. Adjacent to the falls the river splits, forming a small island accessible by a beautiful 55-foot covered bridge. Either enjoy the falls from the short trail around the island or take a quick swim in the cool water below them. There are several picnic areas along the river, a campground with 36 rustic sites (wheelchair-accessible site), and a short wooded nature trail. The rest of the 825-acre park remains wild. The park is on Hwy U, 0.25 mile north of U.S. 2, nine miles southeast of Superior, 398-3000, 399-3111 (off-season). Open first weekend in May to first weekend in October, though winter enthusiasts can still enter the rest of the year. $

Events

The **Fire and Police Muster**, held in mid-July, features a fire and police parade, fire truck rides, demonstrations, live music, craft vendors, a chili cook-off, hot pepper eating contest, and many other heated events.

The **Great Northern Classic Rodeo**, held Labor Day weekend at the Head of the Lakes Fairgrounds, is a popular competition sponsored by the International Professional Rodeo Association. Over $20,000 in prize money is up for grabs in all the popular rodeo events such as bull riding, bareback bronco riding, steer wrestling, team roping, and barrel racing. All proceeds go towards children's needs. Call 218/726-1603 for information or to purchase tickets. $

Spirit of the Lake Fallfest, held the last weekend of September, features a parade, powwow, lumberjack shows, live music, and a large arts and crafts fair.

Shopping

Bibliophiles will want to stop at **J. W. Beecroft Books & Coffee**, the Twin Ports' top independent bookstore. It has a good selection of local titles, a fun children's area, and a coffee shop. Located at 3631 Tower Ave., 394-BOOK. Open daily.

The **Rocking Horse Gift Shoppe** has a large selection of high quality handmade crafts, a large holiday selection, candles, and Wisconsin food items. Located at 310 Belknap St., 392-5141. Open Monday–Saturday.

The **Superior Antique & Art Depot**, located in the historic Union Depot building, offers a truly huge selection of antiques and collectibles from 27 dealers. After you've examined the two floors of the main building, there's still more in the garages out back. Located at 933 Oakes Ave., 394-4611. Open daily. Two other antique stores across town are also worth checking out: **Allouez Antiques**, 4101 E. Second St., 398-0529, is open daily, and **Doherty's Antiques & Craft Shoppe**, 207 Thirty-ninth Ave., 398-7661, is open Monday–Saturday.

The **Wharf Shops** at Barker's Island (p. 75) house a half dozen small stores selling crafts, souvenirs, and snacks. Open mid-May to mid-October.

Performing Arts

Bayside Sounds is a free outdoor concert series held on Wednesday afternoons and evenings from June to September at several locations across the city. Call 394-0299 for more information.

The **Port-Town Part-Time Players**, Superior's community theater group, is currently situated at the Mariner Mall, corner of N. Twenty-eighth Street and Hill Avenue, 398-5462, while they fundraise to buy the old Palace Theater downtown. $

Shack Smokehouse and Grill hosts dinner theater performances every spring and fall, usually in February and October. Located at 3301 Belknap St., 392-9836. $

The **University of Wisconsin–Superior** is the cultural center of Superior offering a wide variety of musical and theatrical performances throughout the year. Most performances take place in the Holden Fine Arts Center at the corner of Catlin Avenue and Nineteenth Street. Call 394-8244 for details.

Golf

There are three golf courses to choose from in and around Superior: The popular, 36-hole **Nemadji Municipal Golf Course**, 5 N. Fifty-eighth St., 394-0266, has received a four-star rating from *Golf Digest* magazine; **Pattison Park Golf Course**, 12 miles south on Hwy 35 then 1.75 miles east on Hwy B, 399-2489, has 9 holes; **Poplar Golf Course**, 13 miles east on U.S. 2 then 1.5 miles north on Hwy D to Golf Course Road, 364-2689, has 18 holes.

Marinas/Charters

The 420-slip **Barker's Island Marina**, 250 Marina Dr., 392-7131, 800/826-7010, is the largest marina on Lake Superior. The full service facility offers transient dockage, sailboat rentals, and a youth sailing program.

Sailboats Inc., 250 Marina Dr., 392-7131, 800/826-7010, in the Ship's Store of Barker's Island Marina, has bareboat or crewed charters. Beginner or advanced sailing lessons are also available.

Several captains dock their boats at the **Superior Charter Dock** on Barker's Island. Call 800/942-5313 for referrals or stop by the dock to pick up brochures.

Bicycling

The paved **Osaugie Trail** runs for 3.5 miles along Superior Bay beginning at the Tourist Information Center and joins up with the **Tri-County Corridor** (p. 79) at its south end. The trail will likely be expanded in the near future. A popular ride is to continue on Moccasin Mike Road to Wisconsin Point (p. 79).

The trails in **Superior Municipal Forest** (p. 79) are open to mountain biking.

Outdoor Rentals

Superior Sports, 310 Belknap St., 394-5600, rents cross-country skis and snowshoes.

Spectator Sports

The **Superior Curling Club** hosts bonspiels from November to

March where you can watch some of the world's top curlers. They also have open houses if you want to try throwing some stones. Located at the Head of the Lakes Fairgrounds, 4700 Tower Ave., 392-2022.

Superior Speedway hosts Friday night (and occasionally other nights) stock car races on the area's fastest 3/8-mile, high-banked clay oval. Races start in mid-May and culminate in mid-September with the Miller Lite Northern Nationals. Located at the Head of the Lakes Fairgrounds, 4700 Tower Ave., 394-7848. **$**

The **UW–Superior Yellowjackets** compete in hockey (the fans' favorite), basketball, soccer, baseball/softball, volleyball, cross-country, track, and golf. Call 394-8193 for schedules and information.

Where to Eat

The **Anchor Bar and Grill**, 413 Tower Ave., 394-9747, cluttered with interesting nautical-related items, may not be for everybody, but if you want tasty food and budget prices then this is the place. In a Best of the Northland readers poll the Anchor won not just "best really cheap food" and "best dive" but also "best burger." Some of the more creative burgers served are the Cashewburger, Hawaiianburger, and the one-pound Galleybuster. They also have a few other sandwiches, such as BLT and grilled cheese. Open daily for lunch and dinner.

Bean's Place, 417 Belknap St., 392-1264, serves pizza, sandwiches, malts and sundaes, and daily specials in a 1950s atmosphere with a classic jukebox. Open daily for breakfast, lunch, and dinner. Delivery is available for pizzas.

The **Galley Restaurant & Lounge** at Barker's Island Inn (p. 84), 392-7152, specializes in fresh seafood, but also has a full menu of steaks, pasta, salads, and sandwiches. The restaurant overlooks the bay and has outdoor seating. Open daily for breakfast, lunch, and dinner.

Lan-Chi's, 1320 Belknap St., 394-4496, has all the usual Chinese options (and some not so usual) plus a selection of traditional Vietnamese food, American favorites, and even Greek gyros. The portions are large, the prices reasonable, and the food is excellent. Open daily for lunch and dinner. Delivery is available. Sharing the same building is **Amigo's Mex Express**, 395-5225, offering fast food Mexican, including some all-you-can-eat options, plus pizza. Open daily for lunch and dinner. It's one of your best late-night options since they don't close until 3 a.m. on Friday and Saturday.

Louis' Cafe, 1602 Tower Ave., 392-3058, has been a Twin Ports standard for over half a century. The large menu features American favorites such as steaks, sandwiches, and salads plus Greek dishes including gyros, spanikopita, and dolmades. Breakfast is served all the time. Always open.

Northern Lights, 1201 Tower Ave., 392-2040, is Superior's newest hot spot. It specializes in steaks, but the menu also includes seafood, sandwiches, salads, stir fries, and sandwiches. Try the portobello mushroom sandwich. Open daily for lunch and dinner.

The popular **Sammy's Pizza–Elbo Room**, 1309 Tower Ave., 392-3829, is known for its homemade Italian dishes such as manicotti, tortellini, fettuccine, gnocchi, lasagna, and of course pizza. The broad menu also includes steaks, seafood, chicken, sandwiches, and salads. Open Monday–Friday for lunch and daily for dinner.

The Shack Smokehouse and Grille, 3301 Belknap St., 392-9836, is a casual and popular supper club that has gained a reputation for its hickory-pit smoked barbecued ribs, pork, and rotisserie chicken. The menu also includes steak, seafood, chicken, sandwiches, salads, and the specialty, prime rib, which is served on Friday, Saturday, and Sunday. Open daily for lunch and dinner.

You'll find the city's best coffees at **Superior Design and Coffees**, 1826 Tower Ave., 392-3303, and **J. W. Beecroft Books & Coffee**, 3631 Tower Ave., 394-BOOK. Both are open daily.

Where to Stay

Bed-and-Breakfast

The Crawford House, 2016 Hughitt Ave., 394-5271, has been restored to its original 1908 splendor. The three guest rooms, including a whirlpool suite, have private baths (one unattached) and feature stained glass windows, natural wood trims, period furnishings, and oriental rugs. Guests can relax in the third floor billiard room with its walk-out porch and are served a full breakfast.

Other Lodging

Barker's Island Inn, 300 Marina Dr., 392-7152, 800/344-7515, adjacent to the marina on Barker's Island, has 115 rooms, including some suites, with cable TV, indoor pool, whirlpool, sauna, game room, and tennis courts.

Bay Motel, 306 E. Third St., 392-5166, has 10 rooms, including a fantasy suite, with cable TV.

Best Western Bridgeview Motor Inn, 415 Hammond Ave., 392-8174, 800/777-5572, has 96 rooms, including some suites, with cable TV, indoor pool, whirlpool, sauna, and free continental breakfast.

Days Inn Bayfront, 110 E. Second, 392-4783, 800/325-2525, has 110 rooms with cable TV, indoor pool, whirlpool, sauna, and game room.
Driftwood Motel, 2200 E. Second St., 398-6661, has 12 rooms with cable TV.
Northland Camping & RV Park, just outside town at the junction of Hwy 13 and U.S. 53, 398-3327, has 60 sites with full hookups, showers, pool, hot tub, sauna, game room, and hiking trails. Open mid-May to mid-October.
Shore Line Motel, 2302 E. Second St., 398-6688, has 11 rooms with cable TV.
Stockade Motel, 1616 E. Second St., 398-3585, has 16 rooms with cable TV.
Super 8 Motel, 4901 E. Second St., 398-7686, 800/800-8000, has 40 rooms with cable TV and free continental breakfast.
Superior Inn, 525 Hammond Ave., 394-7706, 800/777-8599, has 69 rooms, including some suites, with cable TV, pool, whirlpool, sauna, and free continental breakfast.

Camping is also available at **Amnicon Falls State Park** (p. 80) and **Pattison State Park** (p. 80).

Emergencies

Call 911. St. Mary's Hospital, 3500 Tower Ave., Superior, 392-8281.

More Information

Tourist Information Center, 305 Harbor View Pkwy., 392-2773, 800/942-5313, www.visitsuperior.com. The center has tourism information for the entire state.

Duluth Attractions Guide

It's all here. **Canal Park**, nestled along Lake Superior, is the center of tourist activity in Duluth, but it's just as popular with the locals—and seagulls. You could easily spend an entire day here. This reclaimed warehouse district has several hotels, some of Duluth's most popular restaurants, nightclubs, shopping (antique shops abound), and several of its top attractions, all surrounded by sculptures (many by international artists from Duluth's sister cities), fountains, and beautifully restored buildings. Duluth's mounted police are based here and you are welcome to stop by their stable and office at 351 Canal Park Dr. If you want to travel by horsepower, carriage rides are offered May through October. You can swim at the rocky beach by the Endion Station Visitor Information Center.

Your first stop in the park, and the entire city for that matter, should be the massive **Aerial Lift Bridge** over the Duluth Ship Canal. Built in 1905 as an aerial transfer bridge (a suspended gondola moved across the canal) it was modified to its present form in 1930. The central span weighs 1,000 tons and rises the full 138 feet in about two minutes. The bridge, the canal, and adjacent **lighthouses** are listed on the National Register of Historic Places.

The **Lake Superior Maritime Visitor Center**, exploring Twin Ports shipping past and present, is the most visited museum in Minnesota. Among the many fascinating exhibits are a giant steam engine (the engine is hooked up to turn, but it is run only on special occasions), a display showing how the massive ore docks operate, and a pilothouse with hands-on equipment. There are also films, telescopes for ship watching, and computer screens posting ship arrival and departure times. Displayed outside is the tugboat *Bayfield*. Located at the foot of the lift bridge, 600 Lake Ave. S., 218/727-2497. Open daily, April through mid-December, and Friday–Sunday the rest of the year; call for hours. Wheelchair accessible.

It's hard to say who likes **Grand Slam Adventure World** more, kids or adults. The 30,000-square-foot indoor "family fun center" houses, among other things, batting cages, basketball courts, 18-hole mini-golf, Extreme Lazer Tag, bumper cars, video games, billiards, children's play station, and Spaceball, which combines basketball and trampolines. There is also an on-site restaurant. Located at 395 Lake Ave. S., 218/722-5667. Open daily. Entrance is free, but the games cost.

Duluth's **charter fishing docks** are located in Waterfront Plaza Marina at Lake Avenue S. and Railroad Street. Call 218/722-4011, 800/438-5884, for referrals or information.

Across the **Minnesota Slip Drawbridge** Canal Park ends, but the fun on the waterfront continues.

Just across the drawbridge is the **Vista Fleet Excursion Dock**. See p. 76 for details about their not-to-be-missed harbor tours. $

The **William A. Irvin**, the former flagship of the U.S.S. Great Lakes Fleet, which transported coal and iron ore, is now a floating museum. Guided tours lead you through the entire 610-foot ship where you can see the 2,000-horsepower engines, elaborate guest quarters, and cargo hold. Kids love to sit at the wheel in the pilothouse and toot the whistle. During the last half of October the ship is transformed into the haunted "Ship of Ghouls." Docked along Harbor Drive, 218/722-7876. Open 10–4 daily during May; 9–6 Sunday–Thursday and 9–8 Friday-Saturday from Memorial Day weekend through mid-October. $

Docked next to the *Irvin* is the **Lake Superior**, a retired U.S. Army Corps of Engineers tugboat open for self-guided tours. Open same as the *William A. Irvin*. $ or free with paid admission to the *William A. Irvin*.

At the **Duluth OMNIMAX Theatre** you don't just watch a movie, you experience it. The domed screen fills the viewer's entire line of

The Channel Battle

Though it never came to blows, the battle over constructing the Duluth Ship Canal was intense. Prior to the construction of the canal the protected harbor behind Wisconsin and Minnesota Points could be accessed only through the natural Superior Entry, many miles from Duluth but with direct access to Superior. As early as 1857 Duluth business interests promoted dredging a canal to encourage harbor development in their city, but the U.S. War Department opposed the plan out of fear that diverting the flow of the St. Louis River would cause serious shoaling in the harbor. The State of Wisconsin and the citizens of Superior also feared the diversion of commerce the new canal would bring.

In the fall of 1870 Duluth canal backers, undaunted by Congress's denial of funding, began digging their canal and had excavated about two-thirds of the way across the Point before winter arrived and work was stopped. Prominent citizens of Superior, in an attempt to block the canal, went to court, and the next spring the U.S. circuit court issued an injunction. Word reached Duluth on Saturday that the papers would be served in two days. The next day a work crew of about 50 men took to the canal with picks and shovels and completed a small ditch sending a steady stream of water that rapidly enlarged the channel. When the U.S. marshal arrived on Monday small ships were already passing through the channel, which continued to be enlarged by the water's current.

Duluth agreed to build a dike after finishing construction (which resulted in the injunction's being lifted 10 days later), but it was removed shortly after being built as it proved a hindrance to shipping. Litigation continued for several more years as the State of Wisconsin attempted to have the courts order the filling of the canal. Since the effect on the Superior Entry turned out to be minor, the U.S. Supreme Court ruled the canal could stay.

vision, the steep seating offers an unobstructed view, and a state-of-the-art sound system rounds out the experience. Located across from the *William A. Irvin* at 301 Harbor Drive, 218/727-0022, 888/OMNI-MAX. Open daily. Wheelchair accessible. $

Discounted combination tickets for the *William A. Irvin* and the OMNIMAX are available.

Next to the OMNIMAX is the **Duluth Entertainment Convention Center (DECC)**, which features many public events of interest, such as big name concerts, sporting events, and Broadway shows. The DECC is also home to the **Duluth Curling Club** where you are welcome to watch bonspiels during the November-to-March curling season. There are also opportunities for new curlers to step out onto the ice. Call 218/727-1851 for curling information. Wheelchair accessible.

Currently under construction and expected to open in May 2000 is the **Great Lakes Aquarium at Lake Superior Center**. The most highly anticipated display will be the 120,000-gallon aquarium exhibit, only the second freshwater aquarium in the U.S. There will also be interactive historical, ecological, and geological displays about the world's largest lake ranging from its creation to current threats. It is sure to be a must-see. Located at 353 Harbor Dr., 218/525-2265. Wheelchair accessible. $

Bayfront Festival Park is an outdoor venue on the waterfront that hosts some of Duluth's most exciting events, including the annual Bayfront Blues Festival (second weekend in August). In the northeast corner of the park is **Playfront**, a giant playground for kids to explore and enjoy.

The narrow seven-mile stretch of land across the Aerial Lift Bridge is **Park Point** (officially it's Minnesota Point, but you'll almost never hear anyone call it this), the world's largest freshwater sandbar. Because the water is shallow here, and thus warm, this is the Twin Ports' most popular place to swim. The nearest public access to the beach is at Twelfth Street S. across from the Franklin Park Tot Lot, just five blocks south of the bridge.

Park Point Recreation Area has lifeguards on duty plus a beach house with changing rooms and a snack shop. The rest of the park has a boat launch, picnic areas, sports fields, and a large playground with a ship and lift bridge replica for the kids to play on. Located at the end of Minnesota Avenue.

The University of Minnesota–Duluth Aquatics Center offers **sea kayak tours** in the harbor. The tours include equipment and basic instruction; no experience is necessary. It also offers a wide variety of beginner to advanced canoeing and kayaking courses, trips to premier paddling destinations across the U.S. and Canada, and rock-climbing instruction on its indoor wall or at outdoor sites. Located at Fifteenth Street S., next to the U.S. Army Reserve Center. The four-hour tours leave at 12 on Fridays and Saturdays from mid-June through August. Call 218/726-6533 for more information. **$**

You can take a 20-minute **seaplane ride** over the Twin Ports from the Sky Harbor Airport at the end of Minnesota Avenue. Call 218/722-6410 for reservations or information. Flights are available daily, May through September, weather permitting. **$**

The wooded two-mile **Park Point Trail** leads to the very tip of Park Point. Along the way you'll pass many large sand dunes and the ruins of a lighthouse. The trailhead is located next to the airport.

The **Lakewalk** is exceedingly popular with locals and tourists alike. Separate walking and biking lanes hug the shore for three miles between Canal Park (p. 85), where bikes are available for rent, and Twenty-sixth Avenue E. The many benches and picnic tables along the way let you take in the scenic shore at your own pace. The trail passes two interesting sites worth a stop.

The 1885 castle-like **Fitger's Brewery Complex**, listed on the National Register of Historic Places, now houses a hotel, shops, restaurants, and appropriately a micro-brewery. The **Fitger's Museum and Copper Kettle Room** has a small collection of Fitger's brewing memorabilia displayed around one of the original giant copper kettles. A brochure guides you on a walking tour that points out other historical remnants of the brewery that remain in the building. Located at 600 E. Superior St., 218/722-8826. Museum open 10–5 Monday–Friday, 11–4 Saturday, 12–3 Sunday.

Leif Erikson Park is a quiet area with a rocky beach along the lake. The most popular attraction here is the **Rose Garden** (London Road at Thirteenth Avenue E.) with over 3,000 bushes on display. Also of interest is a half-sized replica of the ship used by Leif Erikson when he sailed to North America. In 1926 this boat retraced his route from Norway and ended up on display here.

Officially it's the St. Louis County Heritage and Arts Center, but everyone calls it **The Depot**. And it's one of the Northland's top attractions. The imposing Chateauesque-style Duluth Union Depot building, built in 1892 and now listed on the National Register of Historic Places, houses four museums. The largest and most interesting is the Lake Superior Railroad Museum, which has an extensive collection of vintage railroad equipment that you can climb aboard, including an 1861 wood-burning steam engine (Minnesota's first locomotive), one of the world's largest locomotives, and a rotary snowplow. Other displays include dining car china, railway post office, and track inspection vehicles. During the summer you can take a short trolley ride. Alongside the trains is Depot Square, a re-created 1910 Duluth street scene. The Duluth Children's Museum, one of the first in the nation, focuses on natural history and world cultures. Almost every display is hands-on. The St. Louis County Historical Society's displays focus on northeastern Minnesota with many relics from earlier times, both European and Ojibwe. Finally the Duluth Art Institute has several rooms to host the changing exhibits by regional, national, and international artists. In addition to the museum, five performing arts organizations are based here: the Arrowhead Chorale, the Duluth Playhouse, the Duluth-Superior Symphony Orchestra, Matinee Musicale, and the Minnesota Ballet. Located at 506 W. Michigan St., 218/727-8025, 888/733-5833. Open daily; call for hours. Wheelchair accessible. $

The **Fond-Du-Luth Casino**, operated under a joint agreement between the Fond du Lac Ojibwe and the city, offers blackjack, bingo, slots, video poker and keno, and pull-tabs, for the 21-and-over crowd. There is also a restaurant and bar here. Located at 129 E. Superior St., 218/722-0280, 800/873-0280. Open daily. Wheelchair accessible.

Superior Street, the heart of downtown, is lined with gorgeous historic buildings. Even if you don't want to shop here (there are many galleries and antique stores) you should take time to admire the classic architecture of a bygone era: they don't build them like this anymore. You can use the skywalk system to avoid inclement weather.

The free brochure **"Downtown Duluth: Architecture and Public Art,"** available at the Tourist Information Centers, points out dozens of historic buildings on Superior Street and elsewhere. The one building not to miss, though it would be difficult to do so, is the **Old Central High School** which towers over the downtown. This 1892 Romanesque Revival brownstone, listed on the National Register of Historic Places, has an immense clock tower plus turrets and stone carvings. Located on Lake Avenue at Second Street.

You could also join famous nineteenth-century Duluth pioneer Dr. Thomas Preston Foster (portrayed by a local actor, of course) on a **historical tour of downtown** while he spins colorful tales from the city's early days. The tour departs from the corner of Lake Avenue and

Superior Street at 10 a.m. Saturday from Memorial Day weekend to Labor Day weekend.

Another brochure, **"Walking Tour of Duluth's Historic East End,"** also available at the Tourist Information Centers, is so popular they have trouble keeping them in stock. It details two dozen beautiful, historic homes on Superior and First Streets between Twenty-first and Twenty-fourth Avenues E. They represent just a few of the east end's beautiful buildings made possible by free-flowing turn-of-the-century wealth.

At the **Karpeles Manuscript Library Museum** you can see drafts of some of the world's most famous documents, such as the Bill of Rights and the Emancipation Proclamation, as well as numerous obscure but still important manuscripts. This beautiful old church building is one of seven museums around the nation owned by Duluth native David Karpeles. Only a tiny fraction of the collection, one of the largest in the world, is on display at any one time, but the rotating exhibit changes every three months. It's an invaluable resource for historians, but curious visitors will find it interesting to see documents with items crossed out and changes written in the margins. Located at 902 E. First St., 218/728-0630. Open 12–4 daily, June through August, and Tuesday–Sunday, September through May.

Glensheen, the opulent estate on the shore of Lake Superior, was the home of self-made millionaire Chester Congdon. It was completed in 1908 after three years of construction in which no extravagance was spared, and little has changed since then. The 39-room Jacobean-style mansion still houses the custom-designed furniture, hand-carved woodwork, and leaded art glass windows. Some of the amenities on the surrounding 7.5-acre grounds include formal gardens, a stone bridge over Tischer Creek, and gardener's cottage. Even the carriage house where the horses and cows stayed (and now old carriages are on display) was fancier than most regular homes. The estate is listed on the National Register of Historic Places. Tours take you through the home and grounds. Located at 3300 London Rd., 218/724-8863, 888/454-GLEN. Open 9:30–4 daily, May through October, and 11–2 Saturday and Sunday, November through April. Wheelchair accessible (with some tour modifications). $

The **Tweed Museum of Art**, on the University of Minnesota–Duluth campus, has over 4,500 objects from around the world in its permanent collection. The nine galleries also host many traveling exhibitions and works by faculty, students, and local artists. The museum store has some interesting items. Located next to Cina Hall in the center of campus, 218/726-8222. Open 9–8 Tuesday, 9–4:30 Wednesday–Friday, 1–5 Saturday and Sunday. Wheelchair accessible.

Also on the UMD campus is the **Marshall W. Alworth Planetarium** which has free public shows at 7 p.m. Wednesday while school is in session. Located in Marshall W. Alworth Hall on the south side of campus. 218/726-7129. Wheelchair accessible.

Lake Superior's rugged shoreline at **Brighton Beach** in Kitchi Gammi Park is best suited to picnics or relaxing, but some people also choose to swim here. Located at the far northeast end of Duluth along Hwy 61.

The **Lake Superior Zoo** is home to more than 500 species of animals from around the world with a focus on polar and far north critters. Bubba and Berlin, the zoo's playful polar bears, are top attractions. There is also a children's zoo which offers a hands-on experience, plus a cafe and gift shop. Located at 7210 Fremont St., 218/733-3777. Open 9–6 daily, April through October, and 10–4 daily, November through March. Wheelchair accessible. $

See how paper is made during a one-hour **paper mill tour** at Lake Superior Paper Industries' fascinating high-tech facility. You must be 10 years of age or older; open-toed and high-heeled shoes are not allowed. Located at 100 N. Central Ave., 218/628-5100. Pick up free tickets at the Vista Harbor Dock Tourist Information Center on Harbor Drive. Tours start at 9, 10:30, 1, and 3 on Monday, Wednesday, and Friday between Memorial Day and Labor Day. Call at least 48 hours in advance if you require any special assistance.

Come enjoy baseball the way it ought to be—played and cheered for the love of the game. The **Duluth-Superior Dukes** are part of the eight-team Northern League, an independent pro league considered the equivalent of AA ball. Recent team highlights include winning the Northern League Championship in 1997 and the pitching of Ila Borders, the first woman to play in a professional men's league. The team plays their home games at historic Wade Stadium, at Thirty-fifth Avenue W. and Superior Street, 218/727-4525. The 86-game season runs between late May and Labor Day. Wheelchair accessible. $

The **Skyline Parkway** is a scenic 30-mile drive stretching across Duluth. The marked route roughly follows the ancient Lake Superior shoreline, often rising 600 feet above the present-day lake surface. Scenic overlooks are frequent and, needless to say, they are phenomenal. The central portion passes through the city, but most of the drive leads through forest and along rushing rivers and waterfalls. You can access the east end from Superior Street at Lester Park and the west end on Becks Road near Gary–New Duluth. The popular east portion is known as **Seven Bridges Road**, a narrow unpaved section with not seven but eight stone-arch bridges and the best overlooks. Both the east and west ends are closed during the winter.

Also at the east end of the Parkway, the **Hawk Ridge Nature Reserve** is a 200-acre hilltop natural area owned by the city of Duluth and managed by the Duluth Audubon Club. The main overlook is located one mile east of Glenwood Avenue. People flock from all over the country beginning in mid-August and continuing into December when tens of thousands of migrating raptors follow the air currents along the Lake Superior shoreline on their way south for the winter (best viewing is from mid-September through October between about 9 a.m. and 4 p.m.). As many as 49,000 broad-winged hawks have been counted in just one day. During the migration Hawk Ridge naturalists conduct research and offer free educational programs for the general public. The rest of the year it's still a worthwhile destination for the 2.5 miles of hiking trails and great lake views. For more information call 218/728-5812.

Near the middle of the drive are two parks of interest. **Enger Park**, at Eighteenth Avenue W., should not be missed. A historic rock observation tower rises five stories from the city's highest point. Surrounding the tower are a Japanese garden, picnic area, and several secluded overlooks. The park also has a popular 27-hole golf course. **Chester Bowl**, at the upper end of Chester Park, hosts concerts in the summer and downhill skiing, sledding, cross-country skiing, and ski jumping in winter. It is located at Fifteenth Avenue E.

Port Town Trolley

You can travel between Canal Park, downtown, and along the waterfront on the Port Town Trolley, or use it to take a quick sight-seeing tour. The trolley runs 11–7 (completing a loop every half hour) daily, from Memorial Day weekend through Labor Day, and weekends in September. Wheelchair accessible. $

Duluth has not one but two excursion train trips, each offering a different experience. The **North Shore Scenic Railroad,** with classic engines pulling vintage passenger cars, runs from downtown along the scenic Lake Superior shore. A wide variety of trips are offered: scenic excursions through the city or all the way to Two Harbors, elegant dinner trains with special menus prepared by the chefs of several top restaurants, casual pizza trains, steam train trips, charters, and many special events are also available. Trips depart from The Depot, 506 W. Michigan St., 218/722-1273, 800/423-1273. Trains run daily from Memorial Day weekend to October; charters are available in May. Wheelchair accessible. $ discounted combination tickets are available with The Depot.

The **Lake Superior and Mississippi Railroad** offers a scenic 90-minute, 12-mile route along the St. Louis River. As they say, it's like a "nature walk on rails." The nonprofit, all-volunteer organization uses vintage equipment, or you can ride in the completely open "Safari Car" along the original 1870 rail line connecting the Twin Cities with the Twin Ports. All proceeds are used for the restoration of railroad artifacts and the preservation of railroad history. Charters are available. Trains depart from Grand Avenue at Second Avenue W., across from the zoo, 218/624-7549, at 11 and 2 on Saturdays and Sundays, from mid-June to early September. $

The west side of Duluth has two of the city's most popular bike trails. The **Willard Munger State Trail** is a 75-mile paved route that leads to the town of Hinckley, passing beautiful Jay Cooke State Park (14 miles from Duluth) along the way. It is promoted as the country's longest paved trail and may eventually be expanded to St. Paul or beyond. A shuttle service for bikers has recently begun; call 888/263-0586 for more information. This becomes a snowmobile route in the winter. The **Western Waterfront Trail** is a five-mile gravel path along the St. Louis River that offers great wildlife viewing. Both trails are best accessed at a parking area just south of Grand Avenue on Seventy-fifth Avenue W. You can rent bikes and in-line skates one block away at the Willard Munger Inn, 7408 Grand Ave., 218/624-4814.

Several rivers and creeks rush down the hills of Duluth in a long series of **waterfalls** and rapids before emptying into Lake Superior. The rivers are truly wild in the spring, while later in the year they can slow to not much more than a trickle, but the settings are superb year-round. These rivers form the core of some of the city's best parks, and the hiking trails following these wild and beautiful waterways allow a seemingly wilderness experience. The trails are often steep, of course, but generally easy to follow and undeniably worth the effort. They are listed east to west across the city: **Lester Park Trail**, Superior Street and Lester River Road; **Congdon Park Trail** (the author's favorite), Superior Street and Thirty-second Avenue E.; **Chester Park Trail**, Fourth Street and Fourteenth Avenue E.; **Lincoln Park Trail**, Third St. and Twenty-fifth Ave. W.; **Kingsbury Creek Trail**, 7210 Fremont St. (the trail starts at the end of the gravel road behind the zoo).

Easily visible across the city is **Spirit Mountain** with 23 runs for downhill skiers and snowboarders. Also here are 22 kilometers of cross-country ski trails, Minnesota's longest snowboarding half-pipe, and three tubing runs. Lessons and ski/snowboard rentals are available. Located at exit 249 off I-35, 218/628-2891, 800/642-6377. Open mid-November to mid-April; call for hours. $

More Information

Duluth Convention and Visitors Bureau, 100 Lake Place Dr., Duluth, MN 55802, 218/722-4011, 800/438-5884 voice/TDD, www.visitduluth.com. There are several Tourist Information Centers in the heart of the city: Endion Station in Canal Park; The Depot, 506 W. Michigan St.; Holiday Center, 207 W. Superior St.; and the Vista Harbor Dock.

Chapter 6
Brule-St. Croix Highway
Solon Springs, Gordon, Brule

Lake Superior and the Mississippi River were the two major waterways used by the voyageurs and early pioneers in these parts, and the St. Croix and Bois Brule Rivers, whose headwaters lie just a half mile apart, formed the only direct route between them. The hill separating the two rivers is part of the north-south continental divide which sends the Brule, as it is almost always called, north to Lake Superior while the St. Croix empties into the Mississippi more than 150 miles to the south. Native Americans had used this as a trade route long before the French built forts at each end to control access and support the fur trade.

Today these rivers, cutting across the east and south ends of Douglas County, are still popular travel routes for canoeists, kayakers, and flyfishers who come from across the Midwest to explore and enjoy them.

Solon Springs

This village of 577 people straddling U.S. 53, originally known as White Birch, sprang up around logging and the railroad, the latter making this a popular tourist destination by the late 1800s, but it was water that really put it on the map—and keeps it there today.

Tom Solon, a local entrepreneur, developed a commercial bottling plant in the late 1800s for the local spring water which was eventually sold across the Midwest as Solon Springs Bottled Water. The bottling plant is long gone, but the surrounding lakes and rivers offer world-class outdoor recreation, canoeing and fishing in particular. The village, near the headwaters of the Brule and St. Croix Rivers, sits along 855-acre Lake St. Croix, popular for all kinds of recreation from fishing to water skiing.

Things to See and Do

Lucius Woods County Park, named for Nicholas Lucius who ran the village's first store, is noted for its stand of virgin pine and its giant log auditorium (see p. 97). The wooded 40-acre park in the heart of town has a beach on Lake St. Croix, self-guided nature trail, picnic areas, playground, and campground with 29 sites (11 electric, wheelchair-accessible sites), showers, and dump station. Open mid-May to mid-September.

Across the highway from the park is **Park Creek Pond**, a youth fishing area stocked with trout. Free for children up to 13 years of age.

The **Solon Springs Historical Museum** consists of two buildings. The John Beck Log Home is a hand-hewed, two-story house from 1900 filled with many original and other early furnishings. You'll feel as if you've stepped back in time. Next to it is a new log building filled mostly with old tools. Located at the south end of town at Railroad Street and Jackpine Avenue. Open 1–4 Saturday-Sunday, Memorial Day weekend to Labor Day. Only the new building is wheelchair accessible.

In the south end of the **Brule River State Forest** (p. 102) is the **North Country National Scenic Trail** (p. 98). Seven miles between Hwys A and S have been completed so far and work is proceeding quickly on extending the trail north through the forest; it won't be long before this section is connected to the Chequamegon National Forest (p. 48). The first two miles of the trail, known as the **Brule–St. Croix Historic Portage Trail**, have been here since before recorded history and were the portage used by Native Americans and French traders to connect these two important rivers. It is listed on the National Register of Historic Places. The trailhead is located three miles northeast on Hwy A.

The 4,000-acre **Douglas County Wildlife Area**, known to many as the bird sanctuary, is part of an ancient glacial lake bed and was established to preserve the once common pine barrens and associated wildlife, especially sharp-tailed grouse. The miles of trails and service roads attract hikers, horseback riders, cross-country skiers, berry pickers, birdwatchers, and bird dog trainers, who hold field trials here. Located four miles south on U.S. 53 then 0.5 mile west on Hwy M, which, along with several other paved roads, leads through the area.

Northwest of town on Lyman Lake is peaceful **Anna-Gene County Park** with a small beach, picnic area, playground, boat launch, and a short trail along the scenic northwest end of the lake. The park is located seven miles north on U.S. 53 then eight miles west on Hwy L

> ### North Country National Scenic Trail
>
> When completed the North Country National Scenic Trail will stretch over 4,000 miles across seven states from Lake Sakakawea on the Missouri River in central North Dakota to Crown Point State Historic Site on Lake Champlain in eastern New York. It will be the longest continuous hiking trail in the nation. Currently over 1,500 miles have been certified by the National Park Service since the trail's inception in 1980, and almost twice this many are hikable but not yet certified, though it will be some time before the entire trail is completed.
>
> A 220-mile slice of the trail crosses northern Wisconsin. Over 80 of those miles have been completed so far, and the total is growing fast, thanks to the many dedicated volunteers. Not only does the trail pass through Wisconsin, but both its concept and name originated in the Chequamegon National Forest (p. 48) in the mid-1960s. The 61-mile section through the Chequamegon is now one of the most scenic segments of the entire trail. Other segments pass through Copper Falls State Park (p. 68) and the Brule River State Forest (p. 102).
>
> For more information or to volunteer contact the North Country Trail Association, 49 Monroe Center NW, Suite 200B, Grand Rapids, MI 49503, 616/454-5506, or the National Park Service, 700 Rayovac Dr., Suite 100, Madison, WI 53711, 608/264-5610.

to E. Lyman Lake Road, where you can follow the signs to the park. Open mid-May to mid-September.

The **Douglas County Ski Trail** is a 17.5-mile groomed path through the Douglas County Forest. The trailhead is 1.5 miles south on U.S. 53, by the wayside.

Shopping

The Little Gift House offers crafts with a country motif plus knitting supplies, T-shirts, and a small selection of natural foods. Located on Main Street next to the post office, 378-4170. Open Monday–Saturday, May through December, and Wednesday–Saturday, January through April.

Tom Hassert, the owner of **Wheel Works Pottery**, makes a wide variety of items on site and sells them here. Located on E. Second Street, just off Main, 378-2008. Open Tuesday–Saturday.

Performing Arts

The **Lucius Woods Performing Arts Center** in Lucius Woods County Park (p.97) draws people from far and wide for its outdoor weekend concerts. The wide range of performances includes classical music by the Wisconsin Chamber Orchestra and the Duluth-Superior Symphony Orchestra, as well as country, bluegrass, and even Celtic. Bring a chair or blanket to the performances. For schedules or more information about this volunteer-run organization call 378-4272. $

Golf

Hidden Greens North, five miles east on Hwy A, 378-2300, 800/933-6105, has an 18-hole course.

Where to Eat

Prevost's Cafe, at the corner of U.S. 53 and Hwy A, 378-2287, is where locals go for no-frills family dining. Open daily for breakfast, lunch, and dinner.

For much fancier fare try **Smithy's Supper Club**, one mile north on U.S. 53, 378-2241. It's been here since 1935 so you know they're doing something right. Enjoy steaks, seafood, pastas, and salads plus a great wine list, all with a garden view. Nightly specials include prime rib and frog legs on Saturday. Open daily for dinner.

The **Village Pump** on U.S. 53 at Arbutus Avenue (look for the antique gas pumps!), 378-2212, offers sandwiches, chicken, and pizza in a lively atmosphere. There is outdoor seating and live music on weekends. Open daily for lunch and dinner.

Where to Stay

The **St. Croix Inn**, at the end of Main Street, 378-4444, sits on the shore of Lake St. Croix. There are 32 rooms, including suites, with cable TV, indoor pool, whirlpool, sauna, and free continental breakfast.

Swanson's Motel and Campground, half a mile south on U.S. 53, 378-2215, is a bustling RV park with 60 campsites with full hookups, showers, and outdoor pool. There are also 14 quieter rooms and cozy cottages.

Camping is available in **Lucius Woods County Park** (p. 97).

Emergencies

Call 911. The nearest hospital is in Superior.

More Information

Solon Springs Village Hall, Solon Springs 54873, 378-2235.

Gordon

Antoine Guerdon, whose name was later Anglicized to Gordon, arrived here, where the Eau Claire River joins the St. Croix, in 1860 and stayed until his death in 1907 at the age of 98. He built a trading post for the Northwest Company, which wanted to expand the fur trade with the area's Native Americans. Gordon, who was well educated for his day, is also remembered for setting up a school and church for both White and Native alike.

Eventually the town become a supply point and stopping place on the St. Paul to Bayfield mail route, and hotels and other stores were built. When the railroad passed through and logging began in earnest, the village really began to thrive. Today the village depends less on logging and more on the surrounding lakes, which draw many tourists.

Things to See and Do

The **Gordon-Wascott Historical Museum** is housed in the old Whalen house, which Antoine Guerdon once used to store furs. It now houses a small collection of photos, household items, and animal mounts. Across the street is the 1910 Soo Line depot, which has railroad memorabilia. Located downtown on Moccasin Avenue. Open 10–4 Friday–Monday, Memorial Day weekend to Labor Day. The depot is wheelchair accessible.

Gordon Flowage Park, at the west end of the St. Croix Flowage, is a beautiful 15-acre park with abundant wildlife, and it is the start of the St. Croix National Scenic Riverway (p. 136). It offers some great canoeing on the St. Croix River, or just paddling around the flowage. The park has a picnic area, boat launch, playground, swimming area, and campground with 33 sites (12 electric, wheelchair-accessible sites). Located seven miles west on Hwy Y. Open mid-May to mid-September. Just outside the park is a beautiful picnic area and flowage overlook near the site of a former Ojibwe village.

Events

The people of Gordon go all out during **Gordon Good Neighbor Days**, held the weekend closest to the Fourth of July. There is a voyageur rendezvous, old-time fashion show, fireworks, car show, parades, live music, rubber duck race on the Eau Claire River, mud volleyball, and much more.

Shopping

Pine Square Antiques has a small assortment of furniture and other items. Located on the south side of town along U.S. 53, 376-4355. Open daily, June to early October.

Golf

The 9-hole **Forest Point Golf Course** is located 13 miles east of town at the Forest Point Resort, 376-2322.

Outdoor Rentals

The Tradin Post on the south side of town along U.S. 53, 376-2256, has canoe and tube rentals plus a shuttle service.

Where to Eat

Buckhorn of Gordon, downtown on Moccasin Avenue, 376-2219, is a friendly bar and grill offering basic meals, including sandwiches, pizza, broasted chicken, and a Friday fish fry. Try the one-pound hamburger, if you dare. Open daily for breakfast, lunch, and dinner.

Where to Stay

The **Forest Point Resort**, 13702 S. Crystal Beach Rd., 13 miles east of town, 376-2322, has six log cottages with kitchens on Lower Eau Claire Lake (part of the Eau Claire Chain of Lakes which has some of the last hand-operated locks in the United States). There is a beach, and a boat is included with each rental. Off the water there is a golf course, restaurant, and five-mile cross-country ski trail. Weekly rentals only, mid-June through August.

Camping is available at **Gordon Flowage Park** (p. 100).

Emergencies

Call 911. The nearest hospital is in Superior.

More Information

Town of Gordon, P.O. Box 68, Gordon 54838, 376-2369.

Brule

The small community of Brule, near the middle of the Brule River, is the best place to pick up canoes, kayaks, bait, or anything else you need for enjoying this famous river. The town owes more than just its name to the river; it might have faded into memory without this major destination at its back door. What was once a bustling logging community around the turn of the century, when logs were floated down the Brule to Lake Superior and on to sawmills in Superior and Duluth, now has just a handful of buildings.

The Brule is known as the River of Presidents for the fishing trips here of Presidents Grant, Cleveland, Hoover, Eisenhower, and most notably Coolidge, who spent the entire summer of 1928 at the nearby Pierce Estate on Cedar Island while the official summer White House, housing the executive offices, was in Superior.

Things to See and Do

The narrow, 40,723-acre **Brule River State Forest** encompasses the entire 50-mile Brule River, beloved by paddlers of all abilities and flyfishers. The upper river flows gently, for the most part, while the near constant rapids on the lower river will challenge experts. There are over a dozen access points for fishermen along the river. The forest is topped by nine miles of seldom visited Lake Superior shoreline. You can access this wild area of sandy beach and cliffs at the picnic area at the mouth of the Brule River or at Beck's Road at the far west end of the forest. Most forest facilities are centered around the town. These include 15 miles of trails for hiking and cross-country skiing, picnic sites along the river, and two campgrounds with 40 rustic sites (wheelchair-accessible sites) open March through November. Backpacking is permitted with a free permit. In the far southern end of the forest is the **North Country National Scenic Trail** (p. 97 and 98), which will soon extend to a point near Brule. The forest headquarters is located 0.5 mile west on U.S. 2 then 1.25 miles south on Ranger Road, 372-5678. $

At the **Brule River State Fish Hatchery** you can watch trout in the outdoor raceways or visit the small hands-on interpretive center. Located on Hatchery Road, between U.S. 2 and the forest headquarters (follow the signs), 372-4820. Open daily 8–4.

Brule River Classics can hook flyfishers up with a guide or give neophytes lessons. They also sell all the gear you'll need for a day of angling. Located 0.25 mile south on Hwy 27, 372-8153. $

Shopping

The **Oulu Glass Gallery** is a rather small gallery, but the work as well as the building (itself a work of art) make it worth going a little out of your way to see. If it's made of glass you'll probably find it here, including stained glass items and fused glass jewelry, but it's the unique, multicolored blown glass pieces that will really catch your eye. You can watch Jim and Sue Vojacek blow glass most days during May, November, and December. Located five miles north on Hwy H then 1.5 miles east on Leppanen Road, 372-4160, 888/OULU-WOW. Open daily, May through December.

Golf

Two golf courses are nearby: **Botten's Green Acres**, three miles south on Hwy 27, four miles west on Hwy B, and one mile south on Hwy S, 374-2567, has 9 holes; **Norwood Golf Course**, three miles on south on Hwy 27, seven miles west on Hwy B, and 0.75 mile south on Hwy P, 374-3210, has 9 holes.

Bicycling

The **Tri-County Corridor** (p. 79) passes through town.

Outdoor Rentals

Brule River Canoe & Kayak Rental, on U.S. 2 on the west side of town, 372-4983, rents canoes and kayaks and offers a shuttle service. They also have guided tours to the Squaw Bay sea caves in the Apostle Islands.

Brule River Classics, 0.25 mile south on Hwy 27, 372-8153, rents cross-country skis.

Brule Sports Shop, one mile west on U.S. 2, 372-4849, rents snowmobiles.

Where to Eat

River House Restaurant, on U.S. 2 on the west end of town, 372-5696, is a new family-style restaurant serving steaks, sandwiches, salads, seafood, and daily specials such as prime rib. It also has several Cajun dishes, including chicken and sausage gumbo. Open daily for breakfast, lunch, and dinner.

Where to Stay

Brule River Classics, 0.25 mile south on Hwy 27, 372-8153, has four quaint log cabins with full kitchens and four RV campsites with full hookups. Guest rooms in the beautiful Northwoods-style lodge are available by reservation only; call for details.

The **Brule River Motel & Campground**, on U.S. 2 on the west end of town, 372-4815, has 20 motel rooms. In the back they have crammed in a Finnish cabin and 15 campsites with full hookups and showers.

Camping is available in the **Brule River State Forest** (p. 102).

Emergencies

Call 911. The nearest hospital is in Superior.

More Information

Iron River Area Chamber, P.O. Box 448, Iron River 54847, 372-8558, www.iracc.com.

Chapter 7
Lore of the Lumberjack
Hayward, Lac Courte Oreilles Reservation, Stone Lake

Hayward

Most people either love it or hate it. The myriad of billboards that bombard you as you approach is the first sign that this is a tourist trap and the city of 1,978 people is often an out-and-out madhouse. But Hayward's status as one of the state's premier vacation destinations is secured by the fact that children are among the city's biggest fans, thanks to an abundance of family-friendly attractions.

There really is something for everybody here and some sights are not to be missed, whether you just stop briefly or spend a week. And even if Hayward doesn't sound like your kind of place the surrounding area, with its extensive forests and quiet lakes and rivers, is likely to seduce you.

In 1883 Anthony Hayward, for whom the town is named, formed the North Wisconsin Lumber Company and opened the "Big Mill" at a narrowing of the Namekagon River. The mill, using the most modern equipment, set daily production records and cut as much as 50 million board feet of lumber a year. The company was an instant financial success and Hayward became the prototypical boom town with 1,000 people relocating here in the first year. Lumberjacks descended on Hayward after payday, and like many other Northwoods towns it gained a wild reputation for its gambling, prostitution, and heavy drinking.

As the logging camps closed down in the early 1900s full service resorts were springing up on area lakes. Chicago mobsters were among the thousands of early tourists who were enamored by the tranquillity of the area. The tourists never stopped coming and they remain vital to the economy. The town preserves its lumberjack heritage in its many festivals and attractions.

Things to See and Do

If fishing borders on a religious experience for you, then the **National Fresh Water Fishing Hall of Fame and Museum** is a shrine. But even if you've never cast a line you'll still want to stop here to see the 4.5-story, half-block long musky and climb to the observation deck in its gaping mouth. This is more than just a uniquely shaped building though; it is the world's largest fishing museum. The giant musky and other buildings display thousands of historic fishing artifacts, including boats and motors, rods and reels, trophy fish mounts, and over 5,000 fishing lures. The nonprofit museum also serves as the official qualifier and recorder of world record fish and maintains a research library. There are other large fiberglass fish sculptures on the park-like grounds for kids to play on, plus a video fishing theater, gift shop, and snack shop. Located at the intersection of Hwys 27 and B (you can't miss it!), 634-4440. Open 10–4:30, April 15 to Memorial Day and October 1 to November 1; 10–5, Memorial Day to September 30. Wheelchair accessible. $

Kids just can't get enough of **Wilderness Walk**, which has something for everybody scattered over the 35-acre park. Most popular are the animals (wild and domestic), including tame deer and farm animals strolling around the grounds that you can feed. Other attractions include a western town where you can see a blacksmith shop or pan for gold, a maze, and an arcade. You can have lunch in the cafe or the picnic grounds. Located 2.5 miles south on Hwy 27, 634-2893. Open 10–5:30 (last tickets sold at 4:30) daily, mid-May to Labor Day. Wheelchair accessible. $

If you're not in town for the Lumberjack World Championships (p. 110) you can still experience the excitement at **Scheer's Lumberjack Shows**. You'll see friendly competition between pro lumberjacks in such events as log rolling, pole climbing, ax throwing, sawing and chopping, and even canoe jousting. It's all mixed with history and comedy. Located at the Lumberjack Village, 0.25 mile southeast of Hwy 27 on Hwy B, 634-5010. Shows are held at 7:30 on Monday, Wednesday, and Friday nights, and kid-focused shows are at 2 on Tuesday, Thursday, and Saturday between early June and late August; early and late season shows also are often scheduled. $

From the Lumberjack Village you also can take a unique **historical journey in a 36-foot birchbark canoe**, just like those the voyageurs used during the fur trade. Louie Baron the Voyageur guides you around Lake Hayward while recalling the region's early history in story and song. The 45-minute trips depart on the hour, 10–5

Tuesday and Thursday, June through mid-September. Call 634-5010 for more information or to make reservations. $

Besides being interesting and educational the **Sawyer County Historical Museum** is one of the most peaceful places in Hayward. The museum's two floors house a wide range of historical artifacts and displays, including a pioneer homestead interior, Ojibwe relics, and lots of logging memorabilia. Be sure to see the early two-person chain saw. Located on Hwy B 0.25 mile east of Hwy 27, 634-8053. Open 12–4 Monday–Friday, June through August. The first floor is wheelchair accessible. $

You don't have to eat at the restaurant to enjoy the re-created logging camp at **Historyland**. The log buildings house many turn-of-the-century artifacts, while there is a fully loaded logging sled out front and some old railroad cars in back. There is also a gift shop. Located half a mile east on Hwy B, 634-2579. Open 8–8 daily, mid-May to Labor Day.

Many area businesses try to reel you in with their taxidermy displays, but none compares with the **Wildlife Museum & Bar**, which claims to be "Wisconsin's largest wildlife museum." With over 500 mounts, from hummingbirds to moose, it's probably true. Most of the animals are from Wisconsin, but there are others, including grizzlies and polar bears. Located on Hwy B 0.25 mile east of Hwy 27, 634-3386. Open 9–10 daily. $

Another wildlife display worth seeing is at the **Moccasin Bar** where you can see a former world record musky (67-1/2 pounds, 60-1/4 inches), albino deer, and card-playing critters among others. Located at the junction of U.S. 63 and Hwy 27, 634-4211. Open daily.

Hayward has a plethora of kid-centered recreation facilities. While the kids putt through the 18-hole mini-golf course at **Fiddler's Creek**, their parents can use the driving range with covered tee line or the 3-hole par 3 practice golf course. Located two miles south on U.S. 63 at Timberlawn Road, 634-4108. Open 9–10 daily, May through September. $

The **Hayward Amusement Park** has a 1/3-mile go-kart track and an 18-hole mini-golf course. Located on the south side of town on Hwy 27, 634-3510. Open 10–10 daily, Memorial Day weekend to Labor Day. $

Hayward Mini Golf, has an 18-hole course and a miniature trolley ride for the kids plus a snack shop. Located at Hwys 27 and B, 634-4544. Open 9–9 daily, May to early September. $

Raging Rapids Waterslide is a good place to cool off in the summer. There is also a video arcade, snack shop, and picnic area here. Just next door in the KOA Kampground is an 18-hole mini-golf course. Located 3.25 miles north on U.S. 63, 634-2331. Open 11–7 daily, Memorial Day weekend to Labor Day (limited hours to June 15). $

Another fun spot is the **Hayward Beach and Park** with a small swimming area and boat launch on Lake Hayward. Located at the end of S. Second Street behind the Hall of Fame.

There are two area horseback riding stables. At **Appa-Lolly Ranch**, you can choose a short trail ride, picnic lunch ride, or an overnight camping trip. Located four miles east on Hwy 77, 634-5059. Open daily, Memorial Day weekend to Labor Day, and Tuesdays, Thursdays, and weekends through the fall, weather permitting. $

Mrotek's Stables has 35-minute to two-hour guided horseback rides on wilderness trails, overnight pack trips, and pony rides for the kids. You can also watch local teams compete in Cowboy Polo (using a soccer ball) at 7 p.m. Monday from late June to Labor Day. Located 10 miles east on Hwy 77, 462-3674. Open 9–5 daily, Memorial Day weekend to Labor Day, with fall rides by appointment. $ 10 percent discount before 10 and after 4.

The Namekagon River, part of the **St. Croix National Scenic Riverway** (p. 136), passes through Hayward and offers good canoeing. Also part of the riverway is the **Namekagon–Court Oreilles Portage Trail**, an easy 0.8-mile loop with a boardwalk along the river. This trail is near the end of the historic portage (memorialized by a state historical marker a few miles further south on Hwy 27) used by Native Americans and early fur traders to connect the Namekagon with the Chippewa River. Located 3.5 miles south on Hwy 27, 1.25 miles west on Rainbow Road, and 0.25 mile north on Rohlf Road.

The **Chequamegon National Forest Hayward Ranger Station** can answer all your questions about the nearby forest (p. 48); it also sells guidebooks and field guides. Located at 10650 Main St., 634-4821 Voice/TTY. Open 7:30–4 Monday–Saturday.

The main attractions in the forest in Sawyer County are two all-season trails. The **Black Lake Trail** is a four-mile loop around its namesake lake; an interpretive brochure discusses the area's logging history. The trailhead is located at the Black Lake Campground, 26 miles east on Hwy B, 5 miles north on Fishtrap Road, 3.25 miles north on FR 172, and 0.5 miles northeast on FR 173. $

The 17.4-mile **Mukwonago Trail**, which is especially popular as a cross-country ski trail, offers a choice of four loops. Located 18.5 miles east on Hwy 77. $

Cross-country skiers can also ski the famous **Birkebeiner Trail**. You can access the trail at Hatchery Creek Park, two miles east on Hwy 77 then 0.5 mile north on Hatchery Road, which has 2.5 km of lighted trails for night skiing; or 10 miles north on U.S. 63 then three miles east on Hwy OO, which has 1.5 km of lighted trails. The lights are on until 10 every night.

The **Chippewa Flowage**, or "Big Chip" as locals call it, is a wild and beautiful 15,300-acre flowage with 233 miles of wooded shoreline and more than 200 islands. Despite the many resorts on the lake, almost all of the shoreline remains undeveloped and will always remain so because the state purchased 6,900 acres around the flowage in 1988. Anglers come from across the nation to fish what is widely regarded as a musky factory (this is where Louie Spray caught his world record musky—69 pounds 11 ounces, 63-1/2 inches) but it is also an excellent canoeing spot. There are far too many submerged logs and rock bars to attract pleasure boaters, which keeps the area peaceful for other users. Eighteen free island campsites are scattered about the flowage and provide a prime wilderness experience. Most paddlers stick to the east end of the flowage where they can also explore the Chippewa River. The nearest of the six public boat launches to Hayward is located 14 miles east on Hwy B then two miles south on Hwy CC. For more information contact the DNR at 634-6513.

The easiest way to see the flowage is with **Chippewa Queen Tours**. Hop aboard the fully enclosed *Denum Lacey* for a two-hour, 25-mile narrated tour with Oscar Treland, who lived here before the lake even existed. There are also three-hour dinner tours (24-hour advance reservations required) and private charters. Tours leave from Treeland Resorts, 15 miles east on Hwy B, 462-3874. Departure times are 11 on Monday, Wednesday, and Friday from June through early September; 2 on Sunday from Memorial Day weekend to the first Sunday in October; 2 on Saturday from Labor Day weekend to first Saturday in October. Dinner tours depart at 5 on Wednesday and Saturday from Memorial Day weekend to Labor Day weekend plus Thursdays during July and August. Wheelchair accessible. $

The **Flambeau River State Forest** is a pleasantly remote destination an hour from Hayward in the far corner of Sawyer County. The 90,172-acre forest protects 75 miles of the Flambeau River, whose North and South Forks merge within its borders. The Flambeau offers some of the Midwest's most popular canoeing. The North Fork has long stretches suitable for beginners while the South Fork challenges expert paddlers. There are also several small scenic lakes to explore if you wish. On land are three short nature trails and a 22-mile series of trails ideal for backpacking and cross-country skiing; off-road bikers have their choice of over 100 miles of trails and forest roads, 55 miles of snowmobile trails, and a 40-mile ATV trail. There are also picnic areas and beaches, and don't miss the Big White Pine, a 300-year-old, 130-foot giant. There are two campgrounds with 60 sites (wheelchair-accessible sites) and a dump station plus free canoe sites along the river; backpacking is permitted with free permit. The forest headquarters is located 13 miles east of the small village of Winter on Hwy W, 332-5271. $

Canoe rental and shuttle service are available from the following places on the Flambeau River: **Big Bear Lodge** at Hwy W, 332-5510, and **Oxbo Resort** at Hwy 70, 762-4786.

Scenic Drive

Three marked **Fall Color Tours**, beautiful any time of the year, start in Hayward and loop through the surrounding forest. A map detailing the routes is available at the Hayward Information Center.

The 29 miles of Hwy 77 between Lost Land Lake and Glidden in the Chequamegon National Forest (p. 48) has been designated the **Great Divide National Forest Scenic Byway** (p. 72).

Events

Fishing Has No Boundaries is held the third weekend in May on the Chippewa Flowage (p. 109). The world's first fishing event for disabled persons has grown into a very popular rendezvous with people across the Midwest since its inception in 1988. You must register in advance by calling 634-3185. Volunteers have as much fun as participants.

The **Musky Festival**, held the third weekend in June beginning on Thursday, has been around for half a century. There is much more than just the fishing contests and seminars, though they are a main draw. You'll also find a huge parade, arts and crafts fair, sidewalk sales, three-on-three basketball tournament, foot races, watermelon-eating contest, carnival, and live music.

The world-famous **Lumberjack World Championships** are held the fourth weekend in July at the Lumberjack Bowl. Lumberjacks, and Jills, come from across the world to compete for more than $45,000 in prize money, the largest payout for any lumberjack event. Pros compete in a dozen events including log rolling, pole climbing (if you think going up is something, wait till you see them come down), power "hot" sawing, springboard chop, boom running, and Jack and Jill sawing. Other activities include demonstrations, exhibits, live music, and a trader's camp. Call 634-2484 for advance tickets. $

The **American Birkebeiner** and **Chequamegon Fat Tire Festival**, detailed at Cable (p. 40), have many associated events in Hayward.

Shopping

Antiquity Square Antiques Mall has 20 dealers displaying in a beautiful 1889 brick building listed on the National Register of Historic Places. Located at 108 Florida Ave., 634-5155. Open daily, May through October, and Thursday–Sunday, November through April.

Granny's Trunk Antiques has a good selection of furniture. Located 0.75 mile east on Hwy B, 634-8686. Open Monday–Saturday, May through Labor Day, and Thursday–Saturday until Christmas.

You can find many antiques at the **Hayward Fame Flea Market**, a long-time Hayward institution. Located at the junction of Hwys 27 and B. Open Tuesday and Wednesday afternoons, June–August, and also during big events and holiday weekends.

The **Lumberjack Village Shops** is a little mall with eight log cabin specialty shops featuring a broad mix of clothing, art, food, and gifts items. Located 0.25 mile southeast of Hwy 27 on Hwy B. Open daily mid-May to Labor Day; a few of the shops stay open weekends through September.

At the appropriately named **Main Street Curiosity Shop** you can find that special little something you've always wanted, but didn't know it until you came here. The eclectic inventory includes both new and old items. Located at 214 Main St., 634-1465. Open daily, May to Labor Day; most days, September through December; and Thursday–Saturday, January through April.

Donna Best makes the beautiful pottery at **Pottery at Best**. You'll also find other unique art and gift items. Located at 15845 Second St., 634-6049. Open daily, May to mid-September, and Thursday–Saturday the rest of the year.

Red Shed Antiques is a large multi-dealer facility with many horse-drawn wagons, buggies, and sleighs displayed outside. Located 1.25 miles east on Hwy B, 634-6088. Open daily.

Tremblay's Northwoods Gallery has limited edition prints and woodcarvings, most of it wildlife related. They also do custom framing. Located at 122 Main St., 634-3142. Open daily, May through October; Wednesday–Sunday, November through April.

Everything sold at **Truly Wisconsin** is produced in our great state, but that's about the only thing the eclectic inventory has in common. Items range from furniture to specialty foods to books to artwork. Among the more unique items for sale are birchbark lampshades, cranberry chutney, and snowshoe coffee tables. Located at 113 Dakota Ave., 634-7179. Open daily.

Wood 'n Things has a good selection of country-style crafts, much of it locally made. Located at 238 Main St., 634-3903. Open daily, May through September, Monday–Saturday, October through April.

Golf

Golfers have eight courses to choose from in Sawyer County: **Aken's Golf Course**, 27 miles southeast on Hwy 27, 945-2593, has 9 holes; **Barker Lake Golf Course**, 26 miles east on Hwy B, two miles north on Barker Lake Road, and 0.5 mile west on Golf Course Road, 266-4125, has 9 holes; **Hayward Golf & Tennis Club**, 0.25 mile north of downtown on Main Street then one block west on Wittwer Street, 634-2760, has 18 holes; **Lakeview Golf and Pizza**, 10 miles east on Hwy B, 0.25 mile north on McClain Road, and one mile west on Sandy Beach Road, 462-3787, has a 9-hole par 3 course; **Ross' Teal Wing Golf Club**, 20 miles east on Hwy 77, 462-9051, 800/323-TEAL, has a challenging 18-hole course developed under the Audubon International Signature Course program using some environmentally sustainable initiatives; **Roynona Creek Golf Course**, 0.25-mile north on U.S. 63, 634-5880, has a short 9-hole course; **Spider Lake Golf Resort**, 13 miles east on Hwy 77 then 2.5 miles north on Murphy Boulevard, 462-3200, has 9 holes; **Spring Creek Golf Club**, 2.5 miles south on Hwy 27 then 0.25 mile east on Fun Valley Road, 634-6727, has 18 holes.

Bicycling

The **CAMBA trail system** (p. 42) begins just north of Hayward.

Outdoor Rentals

Hayward Marine, one mile east on Hwy 77, 634-4373, rents boats, pontoons, and snowmobiles.

KOA Kampground, 3.25 miles north on U.S. 63, 634-2331, runs tubing and canoe trips with shuttle service on the Namekagon River.

M & M Rent-Al, on Hwy B 0.25 mile east of Hwy 27, 634-3146, rents canoes, pontoons, boats, and snowmobiles.

Mrotek's, 10 miles east on Hwy 77, 462-3674, rents snowmobiles.

New Moon Ski-Shop, 0.25 mile north on U.S. 63, 634-8685, rents bikes, cross-country skis, and snowshoes. They can direct you to a trail for all abilities and also lead bike rides on Thursdays.

Round Lake Marina, eight miles east on Hwy B, 462-3327, rents canoes, boats, pontoons, and snowmobiles.

Wild River Inn, 0.5 mile south on Hwy 27, 634-2631, has canoe and tube rentals plus a shuttle service.

Where to Eat

Angler's Bar & Grill, 133 Main St., 634-4700, is a fun place to eat. Besides enjoying the homemade pizzas, sandwiches, salads, Mexican items, and all-you-can-eat Friday fish fry, you can also bowl, play video games, or enjoy sporting events on the satellite TV. If the weather is nice, enjoy the outdoor cafe seating in the beer garden out front. Open daily for lunch and dinner.

China House, 15768 Hwy 27/63, 634-7085, serves all your Chinese favorites plus a small selection of American options including steak and BBQ ribs. Open daily for breakfast, lunch, and dinner. Delivery is available.

Coop's Pizza Parloure, 10588 California Ave. (just off Hwy 27/63), 634-3027, has a full menu featuring spaghetti, lasagna, sandwiches, and salads to go along with their homemade pizza. The Northwoods-themed log building has a large aquarium with native fish. It has an all-you-can-eat luncheon pizza and salad bar Sunday–Friday. Open daily for lunch and dinner. Pizza delivery.

Don't let the name fool you, because **Famous Dave's BBQ Shack**, nine miles east on Hwy B, 462-3352, is completely modern in a rustic Northwoods lodge setting with fieldstone fireplaces and small indoor waterfalls. But even if it were run down, people would still flock here for some of the best barbecue you'll find north of the Mason-Dixon line. In addition to the award-winning ribs, the menu includes such tasty items as rotisserie chicken, sandwiches, seafood, and salads. Enjoy views of Big Round Lake and outdoor seating. Open daily for lunch and dinner; breakfast buffet on Sundays.

Historyland Cook Shanty, half a mile east on Hwy B, 634-2579, serves all-you-can-eat lumberjack-style meat-and-potatoes meals in its re-created logging-camp surroundings. Open daily for breakfast, lunch, and dinner, mid-May to Labor Day.

Karibalis ("Karb's"), 212 Main St., 634-2462, has been a local landmark since 1922 when it opened as a bar and pool hall. Best known for char-broiled steaks, the menu also has sandwiches, seafood, chicken, and a large salad bar, while teriyaki stir fry and some Mexican basics add an international flair. Friday has not just a fish fry but a "seafood fantasy" with several options, including walleye, shrimp, and seafood alfredo, while Saturday features prime rib. There is outdoor seating and live entertainment on weekends. Open daily for lunch and dinner.

The award-winning **Norske Nook**, on the south edge of town on Hwy 27, 634-4928, has recently opened a Hayward branch. It serves family-style meals, including sandwiches, steaks, chicken, salads, special seasonal menus, and a Friday fish fry. You can also try such Norwegian dishes as lutefisk, meatballs, lefse, and Norwegian flat bread. After your meal don't miss one of the famous pies, even though it means having to choose from over 32 varieties daily. Everything here is made from scratch, and it shows. Open daily for breakfast, lunch, and dinner.

Tally-ho, 15 miles east on Hwy 77, 462-3646, is an elegant supper club with live piano music on weekends. The menu includes steaks, seafood, chicken, pastas, and broiled lamb chops, a house specialty. There is also a fish fry on Friday, pork prime rib on Saturday, and prime rib of beef all weekend. Open Tuesday–Sunday for dinner.

Satisfy your sweet tooth at **Tremblay's Sweet Shop** where the delicious fudge and many other candies are made on site, as they have been for over three decades. You're likely to find that special sweet you haven't had since you were a kid. Located at 221 Main St., 634-2785, 800/40-FUDGE. Open daily April through December. Mail order available.

For dessert or just a delectable snack head to **West's Hayward Dairy**, 124 W. Second St., 634-2244. The incredible homemade ice cream, made right here, has made it a Hayward institution for half a century. Indoor and outdoor seating available. Open daily for breakfast, lunch, and dinner.

Where to Stay

With well over 100 lodging options to choose from around Hayward, there is truly something for everyone. Despite the abundance of places, it can be tough to find a room at some times during the year. The Hayward Lakes Resort Association, 634-4801, 800/724-2992, can help you find a vacancy.

Bed-and-Breakfasts

The **Lumberman's Mansion**, 15844 E. Fourth St., 634-3012, is a gorgeous 1887 Queen Anne Victorian home built by lumber baron Robert McCormick. Known as the Lumberman's Palace when built, it has been immaculately restored and furnished with period antiques. The five guest rooms have whirlpools and private attached baths. Guests enjoy a full breakfast. Children are welcome.

The **Mustard Seed**, 205 California Ave., 634-2908, is a classic century-old house. There are five unique guest rooms, including a two-room suite, with private attached baths. Some rooms have whirlpools and fireplaces. Guests enjoy a full breakfast. In the back is a cottage with a Jacuzzi and fully equipped kitchen that can sleep six.

Spider Lake Lodge, 10472W Murphy Blvd., 462-3793, 800/OLD-WISC, sits on the north shore of Spider Lake, 20 miles northeast of Hayward. The beautiful hand-hewed log lodge with hardwood floors and cathedral ceilings was built in 1923. The seven guest rooms have private baths, most attached, and are decorated with many original furnishings. One room has a whirlpool. Relax in the large screened porch overlooking the lake or in the sitting room by a fieldstone fireplace. You'll enjoy a full breakfast in the dining room overlooking the lake.

Other Lodging in or near Hayward

AmericInn, at the junction of U.S. 63 and Hwy 77, 634-2700, 800/634-3444, has 41 rooms, including some whirlpool suites, with cable TV, indoor pool, whirlpool, sauna, and free continental breakfast.

Best Western Northern Pine Inn, 1.25 miles south on Hwy 27, 634-4959, 800/777-7996, has 39 rooms, including some whirlpool suites, with cable TV, indoor pool, whirlpool, sauna, game room, and free continental breakfast.

Cedar Inn Motel, at the junction of U.S. 63 and Hwy 77, 634-5332, 800/776-2478, has 22 rooms, some with whirlpool, with cable TV, whirlpool, sauna, and free continental breakfast.

Country Inn & Suites, just south of town on Hwy 27, 634-4100, 800/456-4000, has 66 rooms, including some whirlpool suites, with cable TV, indoor pool, whirlpool, and free continental breakfast.

Edelweiss Motel, 1.5 miles south on Hwy 27, 634-4679, has 8 rooms with cable TV.

Super 8 Motel, south edge of town on Hwy 27, 634-2646, 800/800-8000, has 46 rooms, some with whirlpool, with cable TV, indoor pool, whirlpool, and game room.

Northwoods Motel, 1.75 miles south on Hwy 27, 634-8088, 800/232-9202, has nine rooms with cable TV.

Riverside Motel, 10429 Hwy 27, 634-2661, has 15 rooms on the Namekagon River, with cable TV and free continental breakfast.

Other Lodging Outside Hayward

Cresthill Resort, seven miles east on Hwy 77, two miles east on Twin Lake Road, and one mile south on McClain Road, 462-9911, on the south shore of Lake Placid caters to silent sports enthusiasts. The four simple one- and two-bedroom cottages have kitchens and screened porches, and each includes a boat and private pier. There is also a fully equipped three-bedroom house. Guests have use of the beach, sauna, and playground. A private groomed cross-country ski trail waits right outside your door, and you can use the ski waxing room and bike mechanics area. They also lead guided ski and bike tours.

Grand Pines Resort, nine miles east on Hwy B, 462-3564, is one of the area's premier resorts with unbelievably cozy Northwoods interiors. No detail has been overlooked, though this extravagance does come at a price. The 18 two- and three-bedroom log cabins on Round Lake have stone fireplaces, modern kitchens, and whirlpools, and most have screened porches and private piers. Guests can enjoy the beach or rent a boat or pontoon.

Lake Chippewa Campground, 13 miles east on Hwy B then five miles south on Hwy CC, 462-3672, sits on a large peninsula right in the heart of the Chippewa Flowage (p.109) and is quite peaceful for having 130 wooded sites, 112 with electric and 30 with full hookups, plus showers and a dump station. Amenities available for campers include a beach, playground, volleyball, basketball, ball field, horseshoes, boat launch, game room, and snack shop. Boats, trailers, and a cabin are available for rent. Open May through October.

Treeland Resorts, 15 miles east on Hwy B, 462-3874, on the north side of the Chippewa Flowage (p. 109) has been pleasing guests since 1928, but the facilities are fully modern. The 28 cottages, with one to five bedrooms, have full kitchens, screened porches, and/or decks. The 10 motel suites have full kitchens, separate living room with fireplace, cable TV, and a private deck overlooking the lake. Resort amenities include just about everything you could want: beach, pool, sauna, tennis courts, volleyball, basketball, shuffleboard, playground, game room, paddleboats, boat and pontoon rental, and a restaurant/bar. Treeland also operates **Oak Shores**, six luxury suites with whirlpools, fireplaces, satellite TV, and private piers and decks, on the other side of the lake. Guests here can use all of the facilities at the main resort.

Whiplash Lake Resort, 15 miles east on Hwy 77 then two miles north on Upper A, 462-4302, sits on 500 wooded acres on a private lake. There are three secluded two- and three-bedroom cabins with kitchens and fireplaces. Or you could choose from the two rooms in the classic stone Tudor home, one with separate living room and fireplace. All overlook the lake. More than 11 miles of trails for hiking, biking, or cross-country skiing wind through 150-year-old pines. There is also a beach, playground, and game room above the six-bay boathouse.

Private vacation home rentals on many area lakes are available year-round from **Premier Property Management Company**, 945-3007, and **Property Management of Hayward**, 634-3565.

Three northern Sawyer County lakes—Lost Land, Teal, and Ghost—have been officially designated **"Quiet Lakes"** and have a 10 mph speed limit on the water. These are the only such lakes in Wisconsin, though hopefully others will follow. You can enjoy these peaceful lakes at several resorts, including the following:

Ghost Lake Lodge, 23 miles east on Hwy 77 then 0.25 miles north on Scheer's Road, 462-3939, opened for business in 1935. The 11 simple one-, two-, and three-bedroom log cabins have fireplaces and screened porches; all but one are right on the lake and come with a boat and your own private pier. There are also three modern suites with whirlpools and satellite TV in the lodge and a secluded deluxe cabin. Each unit has a full kitchen. Guests have use of the pool; beach; tennis, volleyball, and basketball courts; shuffleboard; horseshoe pits; playground; and hiking, biking, and cross-country ski trails. A restaurant/bar is in the main lodge.

Lost Land Lake Lodge, 15 miles east on Hwy 77, 0.75 mile north on Upper A, and two miles east on Brandt Road, 462-3218, is a small, quiet resort on this "quiet" lake. The eight lakeside log cabins, with one, two, and three bedrooms, have kitchens, screened porches, and cable TV. Resort amenities include a beach, playground, game room, and restaurant/bar with a renown Friday fish fry. Guests can rent boats, pontoons, and snowmobiles.

Ross' Teal Lake Lodge, 20 miles east on Hwy 77, 462-3631, 800/323-TEAL, is now in its fourth generation of ownership by the Ross family, and the property improves every year. The 22 cottages plus three apartments in the lodge buildings are well spaced along the lake, offering privacy and serenity. The rustic but modern units, from one to four bedrooms, all have kitchens, most have fireplaces, and about half have screened porches. The beautiful 1907 Northwoods log lodge with restaurant is a great place to relax. Resort amenities include a beach, pool, whirlpool, sauna, rec room with games and a piano, tennis, volleyball, shuffleboard, and playground. Guests can also rent boats and pontoons here. Ross' Teal Wing Golf Club lies alongside the resort.

Camping is available at the **Chippewa Flowage** (p. 109), the **Flambeau River State Forest** (p. 109), and the **Chequamegon National Forest** (p. 48).

Emergencies

Call 634-4858. Hayward Area Memorial Hospital, one mile west on Hwy 27/77, 634-8911.

More Information

Hayward Area Chamber of Commerce, P.O. Box 726, Hayward 54843, 634-8662, 800/724-2992, www.haywardlakes.com. The Hayward Information Center is located downtown at the corner of U.S. 63 and Hwy 27.

Lac Courte Oreilles Reservation

Lac Courte Oreilles (pronounced *lock cood ah ray*), a 5,039-acre, spring-fed lake, lent its name to the reservation as well as the band of Ojibwe who live here. The name bestowed upon it by the French means "lake of the short ears" and is assumed to have been chosen because the Ottawa they encountered here did not pierce their ears and use heavy objects to stretch their ear lobes as many other tribes did.

The reservation was established by treaty in 1854, but the area's recorded history began two centuries before this. In 1661 French explorers Radisson and Groseilliers, the first Europeans to travel to the interior of Northern Wisconsin, journeyed south from Lake Superior and spent a harsh winter at a Huron village here and nearly starved to death.

The first Ojibwe settled in the area about 1745 after a child died during the winter hunt and was buried in the forest. The family decided to remain permanently near the spirit of their child, despite the risk of attack by the Sioux, long-time enemies of the Ojibwe. Others followed and several villages soon arose here and the Sioux were driven back.

Today 2,408 people, three-quarters of them tribal members, live scattered across the nearly 48,000-acre reservation. Northwoods Beach, not much more than a collection of vacation homes and a few shops between Lac Courte Oreilles and Grindstone Lake, is the largest community. Most tribal facilities, including the LCO Community College and a health clinic, are located a few miles northeast of here.

Things to See and Do

The **Lac Courte Oreilles Casino** has slots; blackjack; video poker, keno, and blackjack; bingo; and pull-tabs for the 21-and-older crowd. Also here is a restaurant, sports bar, gift shop, smoke shop, and frequent live entertainment and special events on weekends. Located 4.75 miles east of Hayward on Hwy B, 634-4422, 800/526-2274. Open daily. Wheelchair accessible.

The much smaller **Grindstone Creek Casino** has slots; pull-tabs; and video poker, keno, and blackjack. You must be 18 or older to enter. Located two miles northeast of Northwoods Beach at the junction of Hwys K and E (adjoining the IGA), 634-2430. Open daily. Wheelchair accessible.

The **St. Francis Solanus Indian Mission**, established in 1880, makes an interesting stop. The ivy-covered, pipestone church, constructed in 1924, looks as if it was plucked right out of the English countryside. The most noteworthy feature inside is the wigwam tabernacle. There are many nineteenth-century gravestones in the adjacent cemetery. Inside the school is a Native American arts and crafts store that provides an outlet to help preserve many of the traditional skills, such as beadwork and birchbark crafting. There are also beautiful quilts. Some museum-quality items are displayed during the summer but are stored away during the school year for space reasons. Located two miles northeast of Northwoods Beach on Hwy K then 4.25 miles south on Hwy E, 865-3662. Open daily, but you'll often need to find someone to let you in the gift shop.

Though not a tribal enterprise the reservation's most interesting attraction is **The Hideout: Al Capone's Northwoods Retreat and Museum of the Roaring Twenties**. This home away from home is where the notorious Chicago gangster came to relax or to escape the "heat" in Chicago. Guided tours take you through his main lodge built of native stone and wood with its unique spiral staircase and many original furnishings. You'll also see the gun tower, eight-car garage, private jail, and the recently expanded museum. Also part of the complex is a restaurant and gift shop, both detailed below. Located six

The Ojibwe

One of the largest Native American tribes north of Mexico and for many centuries the dominant people in the Chequamegon region, the Ojibwe, also known as Chippewa, arrived here about the same time Columbus made his famous voyage to "the Orient." This became the Ojibwe's primary home after they were forced to flee their homelands at the Gulf of the St. Lawrence River in far eastern Canada because of conflicts with the Iroquois. According to the Ojibwe legend, the Great White Shell "Megis" mysteriously began to drift west and they followed it until it stopped here. During the migration the Anishinabe people split into three, still closely related tribes: the Potawatomi, Ottawa, and Ojibwe.

When the Ojibwe arrived, this area was dominated by the Fox and Dakota, who attacked the newcomers, but they eventually found refuge on Madeline Island which became, and remains, their spiritual home. Sometime at the beginning of the seventeenth century the population grew too large for the island, and during lean winter months the medicine men practiced cannibalism until villagers rose up in defiance and executed them. Fearing the spirits of the deceased they fled the island and spread out across the south shore.

Using firearms obtained from the French the Ojibwe drove the Dakota out of Wisconsin and northern Minnesota. They slowly spread westward themselves and today there are Ojibwe reservations in Wisconsin, Minnesota, Michigan, North Dakota, Montana, Ontario, Manitoba, and Saskatchewan.

Around 1850 the federal government attempted to force Native Americans to move west of the Mississippi River by, among other things, cutting off payments. The Reverend L. H. Wheeler, a Protestant missionary at La Pointe, visited the lands the Ojibwe were to have been relocated to and "returned with the conviction it would be a deed of mercy on the part of the government to shoot the Indians rather than send them to the new region." After the Reverend Wheeler pleaded with the government, it resumed payments and in 1854 signed a treaty with the Ojibwe which assigned them to reservations in northern Wisconsin, where they have remained. See also **The St. Croix Ojibwe**, p. 154.

miles north of the small village of Couderay on Hwy CC, 945-2746. Tours (starting on the hour) are available 12–7 Friday–Sunday in May; daily, Memorial Day weekend to Labor Day; 12–5 daily in September; and Friday–Sunday in October. $

Events

The tribe holds four powwows with Native dancing, singing, and music at Honor the Earth Park located two miles northeast of Northwoods Beach on Hwy K then one mile east on Trepania Road, behind the LCO Ojibwe School. The **Honor the Earth Powwow** held the third weekend in July is one of the largest traditional powwows in the country. Other events that weekend include speakers, veterans recognition ceremony, and a fun run. The other powwows are the **Lac Courte Oreilles Schools Contest Powwow**, late May or early June; **Veterans Powwow**, November; **New Year's Eve Powwow**, December 31. $

Shopping

The Hideout's Gift Shop (see above) with Roaring Twenties era items is a good place to find a unique item for someone special, such as yourself. It also has some high-quality antiques and glassware. Open daily, June through September; Friday–Sunday, October through February and in May.

Hill's Antiques in Northwoods Beach has a good selection. In the attic is a "doll museum" with hundreds on display. Located at 14356 Hwy K, 634-2037. Open daily except Sunday and Wednesday, May through August, and maybe other days in the fall if the weather is nice.

The **St. Francis Solanus Indian Mission** (p. 119) is your best bet to buy Ojibwe crafts, though you'll also find a very small selection in the **LCO casino's gift shop**, which is open daily.

Where to Eat

The Hideout (see p. 119) is also a popular dining destination serving char-broiled steaks, chicken, seafood, sandwiches, and Italian specialties. Prime rib is served on Saturday and Sunday and there is a Friday fish fry. The bar serves several Roaring Twenties cocktails. Open Tuesday–Sunday for lunch and dinner in June, July, and August; Friday–Sunday for lunch and dinner in May and October; Friday for dinner and Saturday and Sunday for lunch and dinner, November through February. You can also get a quick snack in the ice cream emporium between Memorial Day weekend and Labor Day.

Tony's Fireside, in Northwoods Beach on Hwy K, 634-2710, has had several owners since opening in 1932, but it has always been a local favorite. You can enjoy steak, seafood, chicken, pork, and even some Norwegian options, all served in a rustic decor. The roast duck is recommended. Open daily for dinner.

In the LCO Casino is the **Wigwam Restaurant and Buffet** where you can choose from sandwiches, salads, fried chicken, and a few Mexican items on the menu or the all-you-can-eat buffet. Open daily for breakfast, lunch, and dinner, though the breakfast buffet is available only on Saturday and Sunday.

Where to Stay

Lac Courte Oreilles Casino Lodge, 4.75 miles east of Hayward on Hwy B, 634-8574, 800/526-5634, has 56 rooms, including some Jacuzzi suites, with cable TV, indoor pool, whirlpool, sauna, game room, exercise room, and free continental breakfast.

Trail's End Resort & Campground, 1.5 miles east of Northwoods Beach on Hwy K, 634-2423, is located on Lac Courte Oreilles. There are 10 one- to five-bedroom cottages with kitchens and cable TV. Several have screened porches and fireplaces. Two of the units are large, modern "executive-style" homes. The campground has 35 wooded sites with electric hookups, showers, and a dump station. The A-frame lodge has games, a bar and snack shop, sun deck, and fireplace. Other resort amenities include a beach (where you can try log rolling), playground, basketball, volleyball, and horseshoes. You can borrow a canoe or rent a boat or pontoon.

Emergencies

Call 634-4858. The nearest hospital is in Hayward.

More Information

Lac Courte Oreilles Tribal Governing Offices, 13394 W. Trepania Rd., Bldg. 1, Hayward 54843, 634-8934.

Stone Lake

The quiet village of Stone Lake, just 15 minutes south of Hayward, is a peaceful alternative to the hustle and bustle of its larger neighbor. The town was originally located across the county line directly on Stone Lake, which lent its name to the settlement. In 1887 the town moved to higher ground in Sawyer County where a large sawmill cut millions of board feet of timber from the surrounding forests. Today the village is known for its cranberries. Wisconsin is the nation's leading cranberry producer, supplying 40 percent of the entire U.S. crop.

Things to See and Do

The one-room **Stone Lake Area Historical Museum** in the former Stone Lake Town Hall, built in 1921, has a small collection of historical artifacts and pictures commemorating the area's history. Located 0.5 mile north on Hwy 70, 2.5 miles west on Hwy A, and 0.25 mile northeast on Slayton Road, 865-2519. Open 1–4 Sundays, Memorial Day weekend to Labor Day. Wheelchair accessible.

Scenic Drive

Lake Road and Little Stone Road hugging the west shore of Stone Lake for just over two miles have been officially designated **Wisconsin Rustic Roads**. Though somewhat scenic it's not worthy of this designation since there are houses along the entire route.

Events

Celebrate the cranberry harvest at the **Stone Lake Cranberry Festival**, held the first weekend in October. Activities centering on this tart little berry include cranberry marsh tours, cranberry crate derby, cranberry baking contests, and cran-foods ranging from pancakes to ice cream sundaes and cran-dogs to donuts. There is also an arts and crafts fair, flea market, live music, carnival, horseshoe tournament, and a parade.

Shopping

The Cottage Shops of Stone Lake have mostly small craft and gift items, much of it locally made. They also have some antiques. Located at the corner of First Street S. and Gibson Avenue, 865-5049. Open Thursday–Monday, May through October.

The Last Frontier has a large selection of many different items and all of it is really nice. You'll find antiques, crafts (including a holiday room), Wisconsin foods, and many creative hand-woven baskets. Located in town on Hwy 70, 865-3302. Open daily, April through October, and limited hours in November and December.

Old Stone Lake Village, in a Swedish-style log cabin, has a good selection of antiques; they also sell and store fine wines in the wine cellar and host wine tastings. Located just south of town on Fourth Street S., 865-6060. Open daily, May–October and weekends in December.

Reflections of the Past has a small collection of antiques and collectibles. Located half a block east of Hwy 70 on Main Street, 865-5505. Open Friday–Monday, May–October, plus Wednesday and Thursday in July and August.

Things Remembered has a large selection of depression-era glass items. Located three miles southwest on Hwy 70 then 0.25 mile north on Dawn Street, 865-5600. Open daily April–December.

Where to Eat

The **Loon Cafe**, on the north side of town on Hwy 70, 865-3111, offers basic family dining with sandwiches, salads, homemade soups and pies, and breakfast served all day. There are daily specials including an all-you-can-eat Friday buffet featuring fish, chicken, and shrimp from May to early October. Open daily for breakfast and lunch plus Fridays for dinner.

Maximilian Inn, 3.25 miles east on Hwys 27/70, 865-2080, features fine German dining, and since the owner was born and raised in Bavaria, you can expect top quality meals. German dishes include sauerbraten, roast duck, and several varieties of schnitzels. You'll also find steak, seafood, and lamb chops on this meat lovers' menu. The daily specials include a Friday fish fry, Saturday prime rib, and Sunday barbecued ribs. Open for dinner daily, Memorial Day weekend to mid-October, and Wednesday–Saturday the rest of the year.

Where to Stay

Bed-and-Breakfasts

The **Lake House**, 5793 Division Ave., 865-6803, is a 1917 country home on Stone Lake. All but one of the four guest rooms have private attached baths and one has a gas fireplace and a private deck. You can relax fireside in the hearth room, watch a sunset from the enclosed porch, swim in the sandy beach, or paddle around the lake in their canoe. Guests also have use of a bike storage area and ski-waxing room. A full breakfast is served in the dining room overlooking the lake.

New Mountain, W16199 Musky Point Dr., 865-2486, 800/NEW-MT-BB, sits on a hill overlooking Big Sissabagama Lake, seven miles south of town. The charming home with a European touch has five guest rooms: one with private attached bath, one with private unattached bath, and three that share two baths. After hiking or skiing the trail through the wooded grounds or paddling around one of the area lakes you can unwind outside on the deck, in front of a fire in the Great Room, on a pontoon, or best of all, in the sauna. Children are welcome and will love the petting farm on the grounds. Guests enjoy a full breakfast.

Randall's Morningside, 6138 N. Morningside Ln., 865-2213, sits on the north shore of Whitefish Lake, five miles east of town. With nearly as many windows as walls this modern home really makes use of its lakeside setting. The three guest rooms have one private unattached and one shared bath. You can relax outside on the quiet porch or in front of the fieldstone fireplace. A full breakfast is served in the dining room overlooking the lake.

Emergencies

Call 634-4858. The nearest hospital is in Hayward.

More Information

Stone Lake Area Tourism Information, Rt. 1, Box 73C, Stone Lake 54876, 639-6822.

Chapter 8
Land of 1,000 Lakes
Spooner, Shell Lake, Trego, Birchwood

Spooner

Spooner came into existence at a spot known as the Great Omaha X, where the Chicago, St. Paul, Minneapolis, and Omaha Railway lines crossed as they headed to Hudson, Eau Claire, Superior, and Ashland. Eventually one could catch a train in five different directions (a branch line also ran to Park Falls) from Spooner, making it one of the busiest railroading cities in the north.

The railway platted the town here in 1883, moving its operations about two miles south from a community called Chandler. The new location had several advantages, principally a better supply of water. They named the town after John Coit Spooner, a prominent railroad attorney—who fought progressive reforms in railroad law and prevented undeveloped railway land from being returned to the public domain—and later a U.S. senator. With the exception of a historic excursion railroad, no more trains run through this city of 2,566, but three busy highways converge here, keeping passenger traffic high.

Things to See and Do

The **Railroad Memories Museum**, housed in the 1902 Chicago and North Western Railway depot, is literally packed with vintage railroading memorabilia. If you read all the labels you'll learn a lot, but it's also enjoyable to just browse at the many interesting items. The extensive collection includes track inspection vehicles, signs and signals, train car interior displays, track workers' tools, old uniforms, railroad art, running model trains, railroading videos, and much more. The volunteers who work at this nonprofit museum include many retired railroad employees who really know their stuff. Located on N. Front Street at Oak Street, 635-2752. Open 10–5 daily, Memorial Day weekend to Labor Day. Wheelchair accessible. $

Take a trip back in time on the **Wisconsin Great Northern Railroad**, which departs from the museum. A vintage 1940 locomotive escorts the mahogany-adorned passenger cars from 1912 and 1918 on the 14-mile round trip to Trego (p. 135). You can return on a later train if you wish to spend some time in Trego. They also have evening pizza trains and dinner trains, which require reservations. The excursion trains depart at 11, 1, and 3 (additional departures during special events) on Saturday and Sunday in April; Friday–Sunday in May, June, and September; and daily in July and August. Call 635-3200 or 888/390-0412 for reservations or more information. $

The **Governor Tommy G. Thompson State Fish Hatchery** is the world's largest cold water hatchery producing roughly 2 million walleye and 100,000 musky each year between April and October. The visitor center has hands-on displays about fish, habitat, and the hatchery process, while observation windows allow you to see the incubation area. Out front is a show pond where several species of fish found in Wisconsin are easily visible. The adjacent Fish Hatchery Park has a wheelchair-accessible fishing pier on the Yellow River Flowage and accessible platforms on the river plus a boat launch and picnic area. Located at 951 W. Maple St. (Hwy 70), 635-4147. Open 8–4 Monday–Friday, guided tours at 10 and 2 during April and May, rest of the year by request. Wheelchair accessible.

Snowmobiling

No place loves snowmobiling more than northern Wisconsin, though it's not too surprising considering the vehicle was invented here. Beginning with the first substantial snowfall an impressive winter highway system with road signs, advertising, and bridges is laid out across the state. Many businesses advertise what trail they are located on and set up parking lots for riders. Even schools make arrangements for students driving their own sleds. These six counties alone have over 2,000 miles of marked and maintained trails. Most of these are maintained by local snowmobile clubs, but local and state governments recognize the importance to the economy of the thousands of riders who descend on the Northwoods and also pitch in.

Bulik's Amusement Center has a go-kart track, two waterslides, 18-hole mini-golf course (in the shade), arcade, and batting cage for the kid in all of us. There is also a picnic area with grills. Located a half mile north on U.S. 63, 635-7111. Open 9–9 daily, Memorial Day weekend to Labor Day, and weekends into October. $

Cross-country skiers have two local options. The 4.9-mile **Beaver Brook Trail** is two miles east on Hwy 70 then 2.5 miles south on Cranberry Marsh Road. In town, at the north end of College Street, is the 1.2-mile **College Street Park Ski Trail**. Both trails are groomed.

Events

The biggest event to hit Spooner each year is the **Heart of the North Rodeo**, held the second weekend in July at the Washburn County Fairgrounds. This PRCA-sanctioned pro rodeo event has $40,000 in prize money up for grabs in the seven events held each day: bull riding, saddle bronc riding, calf roping, girls' barrel racing, steer wrestling, bareback riding, and team roping. Other activities that weekend include a rodeo parade, cowboy church service, country music, 10k run, and the Exceptional Rodeo for children with special needs who partake in rodeo-style events. Call 800/367-3306 to purchase advance tickets. $

Railroad Heritage Days, held in June or July, celebrates the area's railroad history. Events, including train rides, equipment demonstrations, model train show, railroad art exhibit, Casey Jones Day at local restaurants (serving food from "the good ol' days"), kiddie parade, and live traditional music are centered on the Railroad Memories Museum.

Jack Pine Savage Days, held the first weekend in August, celebrates the days of yore with log rolling and other lumberjacking competitions and demonstrations. A motley group of local men spend weeks preparing their beards and image for the honor of being named Mr. Jack Pine Savage. There is also a carnival, arts and crafts fair, live music, fun run/walk, and sporting events.

Shopping

Antique Associates Mall is a large multi-dealer facility. Located at 220 Walnut St., 635-6666. Open daily.

Adjoining Antique Associates is **Dahl's Home Store**, 635-2927, which sells not only furniture but also a huge selection of country-style crafts. Open daily, Memorial Day weekend to Labor Day, and Monday–Saturday the rest of the year.

Dunk's Art Barn and Collectibles has filled the lower level of its barn with antiques and hand-crafted furniture, arts and crafts, and quilts made by local artisans. Located three miles east on Hwy 70, 635-2629. Open daily, May to October.

Poor Richard's Antiques is an old house filled to the ceiling, and then some, with antiques. There is a large selection of used books. Located at 202 Balsam St. (along U.S. 63), 635-8747. Open Monday–Saturday, April through October.

The Spooner General Store draws most people in for its candy and fudge, but it also sells coffees and an eclectic mix of gifts from stationery to toys and games. Located at 218 Walnut St., 635-6487. Open Monday–Saturday plus Sundays from Memorial Day weekend to Labor Day.

Golf

The **Spooner Golf Club**, one mile north on U.S. 63 then 1.5 miles east on Hwy H, 635-3580, has 18 holes.

Outdoor Rentals

Riverbrook Bike & Ski, 102 E. Maple St., 635-2134, rents bikes, cross-country skis, and snowshoes.

Where to Eat

The Beanery, 705 S. River St., 635-7699, named after the original 1903 restaurant in the old Spooner Depot, features sandwiches, steaks, salads, and other classic American fare, plus a couple of Mexican options. Daily specials have included shrimp jambalaya, stir fries, and a Sunday lunch buffet. After dinner try to decide from the dozens of dessert options. Open daily for breakfast, lunch, and dinner.

Foxxy's, one mile west of U.S. 63 on Elm Street, 635-2399, has a broad menu including steak, prime rib, chicken, seafood, salads, pastas, stir fries, chimichangas, and pizza. Open daily for dinner.

Macias' Authentic Mexican Restaurant, 129 Walnut St., 635-4510, is a small and simple restaurant serving good Mexican food. Open daily for lunch and dinner, May to Labor Day; Monday–Saturday for lunch and Friday-Saturday for dinner the rest of the year.

Sam Hicks, 921 River St., 635-9119, serves up the food fast, but this is not your average fast food. The menu has a variety of items such as pitas, subs, burritos, and pizzas-for-one, all made while you wait and without chemicals and preservatives. There is outdoor seating and a small dining room. Open daily for lunch and dinner, mid-April through November.

Where to Stay

Bed-and-Breakfast

The **Green Valley Inn**, N4781 Julie Ann Blvd., 635-7300, a small hand-hewed log home, is in a quiet country setting one mile southwest of Spooner. The guest room has a private attached bath and loft sitting room. A full country-style breakfast is served at your convenience. Open May through October.

Other Lodging

American Heritage Inn, 101 W. Maple St., 635-9770, 800/356-8018, has 45 rooms (some have whirlpool and one has a kitchen) with cable TV, indoor pool, whirlpool, sauna, game room, and free continental breakfast.

Country House, 717 S. River St., 635-8721, 800/715-8721, has 22 rooms with cable TV, indoor pool, whirlpool, and indoor golf. There are 21 RV sites with full hookups in back.

Green Acres Motel, 4809 U.S. 63 S, 635-2177, 800/373-5293, has 21 rooms with cable TV.

Inn Town Motel, 801 River St., 635-3529, 800/652-1422, has 20 rooms with cable TV.

Sandman Motel, 4848 Hwy 253, 635-3535, has 18 rooms, one with a kitchen, with cable TV.

Emergencies

Call 911. Community Memorial Hospital, 819 Ash St., 635-2111.

More Information

Spooner Chamber of Commerce, 122 N. River St., Spooner 54801, 635-2168, 800/367-3306. There is an albino buck on display here.

Shell Lake

Shell Lake, from which the city of 1,260 people took its name, is the largest land-locked, spring-fed lake in Wisconsin. The 2,600-acre lake was known as *Mokokeses Sahkiagin* (frog's navel), by the Ojibwe. They bestowed this name upon it since the shallow, muddy lake produced no fish or wild rice, just frogs. U.S. Government surveyors in the middle of the century changed it slightly to Frog Lake. Its final name came not from armored fauna but from the lake's contour. Today it's no longer barren and fishing is a popular pastime, particularly walleye and musky.

The town got its start as a simple trading post in 1872 at about the time logging operations began in the area. Soon after the railroad arrived, a lumber mill was built and the town, which was then known as Summit, grew rapidly. When logging ended many people left, but enough people were able to farm the cutover land that the town survived and is now the county seat.

Things to See and Do

The **Washburn County Historical Museum** displays a wide range of memorabilia in four historic buildings. The main building is the 1888 St. John's Lutheran Church, which retains its original carved wood altar. Don't miss the 1939 hair permanent machine—it looks like something out of Frankenstein's laboratory. The parsonage house next door is the museum annex. In back is the Beaver Brook School, a turn-of-the-century one-room schoolhouse, and the tiny building is a World War II "Sky Watch" observation post for spotting enemy planes. Located at 102 Second Ave., 468-2982. Open 10–4 Wednesday–Saturday, Memorial Day weekend to Labor Day. Some areas are wheelchair accessible.

The **Museum of Woodcarving** houses the world's largest collection of woodcarvings created by one man. This interesting folk art obsession consists of nearly 100 life-sized statues telling the story of the Bible with the main feature being a re-creation of Leonardo da Vinci's *Last Supper*. It took Joseph Barta, a Spooner schoolteacher, over four years to create just this one. There are also hundreds of other small carvings of various themes: look for the dancing monkeys and elephants. Located just north of town on U.S. 63, 468-7100. Open 9–6 daily, May through October. Wheelchair accessible. $

The **Shell Lake Public Beach and Park** is a popular spot to cool off. Besides the supervised beach there is a picnic area, playground, basketball court, and paddle boat rental at the snack shop. Off the shore is a raft with a diving board. Located at the edge of downtown along U.S. 63 at Fifth Avenue.

The **Sawyer Brook Springs Ski Trail** is a wooded five-mile groomed trail at the north end of town. The trailhead is located at the north end of First Street.

The **Hunt Hill Audubon Sanctuary**, owned by the National Audubon Society but operated by a local group, is an environmental education center offering classes in outdoor skills and nature appreciation. Day visitors can enjoy more than four miles of beautiful hiking trails winding through the 500-acre preserve's forest, prairie, wetlands, and lakes. This is a great place to observe wildlife, especially birds. Located one mile south on U.S. 63, eight miles east on Hwy D, 0.5 mile north on Hwy P, and three miles east on Audubon Road. For a program schedule or other questions call 635-6543. Use of trails is free (donations appreciated), but most programs have a fee.

Events

Scandinavian Saturday, held the second Saturday in August at Shell Lake High School, celebrates Scandinavian culture with authentic crafts, food, music, and exhibitions.

The town's biggest bash is **Town and Country Days**, beginning the Thursday before Labor Day and continuing through the long weekend. Enjoy carnival rides; chain saw and crosscutting contests; parades; horse, tractor, and kiddie tractor pulls; bike and foot races; sailboat regatta; arts and crafts; spelling bee; sports tournaments; and live music.

Shopping

The **Antique and Gift Mall** and **Jean's Antiques** are two packed antique stores right next to each other downtown. Located at 24 and 32 Fifth Ave. respectively, 468-7035. Open Monday–Saturday, March through December, and Thursday–Saturday in January and February.

Stop by the **Maple Syrup Ranch** to buy the best maple syrup you've ever tasted. You can also get maple candy and Margo's incredible cornhusk dolls. They gather, boil, and bottle their own syrup and you can tour the production center, a mix of modern and old, and learn every last detail of the process from the tree to the jar. The sap is usually running from late February into April. Located one mile north on U.S. 63, 468-2251. Open daily.

Schaefer Apiaries, a working bee farm, sells pure beeswax candles, maple syrup, gift items, and honey, It's worth a visit just to see the free beekeeping exhibit with an indoor hive behind a glass case. Located 1.5 miles north on U.S. 63, 468-7484. Open Monday–Saturday, May through December.

Thunder Gift Gallery, has mostly Native American–themed jewelry, crafts, blankets, and art from the Southwest, Northwest, and Northwoods. Located at 453 U.S. 63, 468-4477. Open April through January.

Performing Arts

The University of Wisconsin's **Indianhead Arts & Education Center** holds concerts by students and teachers on Friday nights from June to August. Free informal concerts are sometimes held on other nights as well. Located at 802 First St., 468-2414. $

Golf

There are three golf courses near town: **Barronett Hills Golf Course**, seven miles south on U.S. 63 to Barronett then half a mile north on Old Hwy 63, 468-7184, has 9 holes; **Butternut Hills Golf Club**, 11 miles east on Hwy B, 635-8563, has 18 holes; **Clam River Golf Club**, one mile south on U.S. 63 then 6.5 miles west on Hilltop Road, 468-2900, has 9 holes.

Outdoor Rentals

Shell Lake Water Sport Rental, on U.S. 63 across from the Shell Lake Beach, 468-2008, 888/468-2018, rents pontoons, boats, wake boards, tubes, and other items to expand your enjoyment on the lake. They will deliver.

Where to Eat

The **Classic Cafe**, 403 U.S. 63, 468-2969, offers sandwiches, salads, chicken, and daily specials in their dining room plus walk-up service for ice cream treats. Open daily for breakfast and lunch, plus dinner May through September.

Where to Stay

Bed-and-Breakfast

Maple Syrup Ranch, N3534 U.S. 63, 468-2251, is plain on the outside, but Rollie and Margo Schaefer make it warm and inviting inside. This is a working maple syrup operation, hence the name, in a quiet, rural setting. There are two antique-filled guest rooms with unattached baths. A full breakfast—featuring maple syrup, of course—is served in the morning.

Other Lodging

Aqua Vista Motel, 412 E. Hwy B, 468-2256, 800/889-2256, has 18 basic rooms, some with kitchens, and a beach on Shell Lake.

Lakeview Hotel, 105 Fifth Ave., 468-2595, has 19 old-fashioned hotel rooms with shared baths and cable TV.

Marawaraden Resort, N1728 Hwy M, 354-3855, 12 miles east of town on Long Lake, has 13 rustic one-, two-, and three-bedroom cottages with cable TV. Each unit comes with its own boat and a charcoal grill and some have extras, such as kitchen facilities, fireplace, and even a sauna. You can splash around the beach or rent a pontoon to cruise the lake. There is a grocery store on the premises. Weekly rentals only during the summer.

The **Shell Lake Municipal Campground**, located at the edge of downtown on U.S. 63 next to the public beach, has 41 RV sites with full hookups, showers, and a dump station.

Emergencies

Call 911. Indianhead Medical Center, 113 W. Fourth St., 468-7833.

More Information

Shell Lake Chamber of Commerce, P.O. Box 121, Shell Lake 54871, 800/367-3306.

Land O' Lakes

Lake Superior may be the dominant body of water here, but it's hardly alone. Wisconsin has 15,057 lakes, over 3,200 more than Minnesota, if you're keeping track. Bayfield and Washburn Counties each have nearly a thousand lakes; Burnett, Douglas, and Sawyer weigh in with about 500 per county; while Ashland County is almost bone dry with a meager 157.

Trego

Highways 53 and 63 keep this tiny town on the map by funneling motorists through who stop to eat, fill up their gas tanks, or shop for gifts and antiques. But it is a quieter, much more scenic highway, the Namekagon River, that prompts people to stay. Not only is this one of the top canoeing rivers in the Midwest, but downstream from here is one of the wildest and most popular stretches of the St. Croix National Scenic Riverway (p. 136).

This town was originally called Superior Junction since this is where the rail line branched off to Superior and Hayward. It was changed to Trego (pronounced *tree-go*) in 1902 for a reason that depends on which story you believe: trains could go in three different directions from here, or people watching trees shipped by rail to mills came up with a descriptive name.

Things to See and Do

Besides providing all the information you'll need for a trip on the **St. Croix National Scenic Riverway** (p.136), the **Namekagon Visitor Center** has historical and ecological exhibits, including hands-on displays for kids and a slide program. Located half a mile east on U.S. 63, 635-8346. Open 8–4:30 daily, Memorial Day weekend to Labor Day, and weekends in May and September. Wheelchair accessible.

Two riverway hiking trails are located nearby. The 2.5-mile **Trego Nature Trail** starts 0.25 mile east of the visitor center and leads along the high banks above the Namekagon River. The 3.6-mile **Trego Lake Trail**, which is groomed for cross-country skiing in the winter, is located one mile north on U.S. 53 then two miles west on North River Road.

Hay Lake Ranch offers short trail rides as well as full-day and overnight horseback riding trips. Pony rides are available for small children. Located six miles north on U.S. 53, 7.5 miles east on Hwy F, and one mile north on Hay Lake Road, 766-2305. Open 9:30–4:30 daily, May through October. $

The **Springbrook Church Museum**, operated by the Washburn County Historical Society, is located in the restored 1906 St. Magdalene Catholic Church, a classic small town building. Besides church artifacts there are also historic photos, medical displays, old farm tools, and railroad artifacts. It makes a good stop if you're on your way to Hayward. Located eight miles east on U.S. 63, the museum is one block off the highway, 766-3876. Open 11–4 Friday-Saturday, June

> ## St. Croix National Scenic Riverway
>
> The St. Croix National Scenic Riverway includes two of the most pristine rivers in the country, the St. Croix and the Namekagon (nah meh kah gun). Established in 1968 as one of the original projects in the National Wild and Scenic Rivers System, the riverway has become one of the Midwest's premier canoeing destinations. With only class I rapids, except during high water periods, both rivers are ideal for novice paddlers. Canoe rentals and shuttles can be found all along the riverway.
>
> The 154-mile stretch of the St. Croix within the Riverway starts at Gordon Flowage Park (p. 100) near Gordon, and the 98-mile Namekagon begins in the Chequamegon National Forest (p. 48) near Cable. Most sections have sufficient water levels for canoeing all season except for the upper stretches of each river (the St. Croix above the CCC Bridge Landing, a few miles upstream from its confluence with the Namekagon, and the Namekagon above Hayward), which are best run in the spring. The Riverway continues beyond Burnett County all the way to the Mississippi River, though the farther you go downstream beyond here the more likely you are to share the river with motorboats.
>
> There are over 100 free campsites along the rivers. Only designated sites may be used and there is a one-night-per-site limit above Nevers Dam near the town of St. Croix Falls. All of the area covered by this guide falls under these limits. The National Park Service also maintains several hiking and cross-country ski trails along the river which are described in this book with the nearest community. For maps or other information contact the St. Croix National Scenic Riverway, P.O. Box 708, St. Croix Falls 54024, 483-3284, or stop by one of the visitor centers in Trego (p. 135) or near Grantsburg (p. 143).

through August.

Shopping

The two antique stores in town are **Attic Antiques & Collectibles**,

635-6634, which has a large and varied selection, and **Brewer's Trego Crossing Antiques & Collectibles**, 635-8446, which has a little of everything but specializes in hunting and fishing collectibles. Both are located behind the Dinner Bell Restaurant and are open daily.

Namekagon Outpost is a large log building packed with high quality art, log furniture, and more, most with an outdoor theme. Unique items include chain saw carvings, giant barrel saunas, and hand-crafted snowshoes. Located at the junction of U.S. 53/63, 635-7569. Open daily.

Schooltime Antiques in the nostalgic 1924 Earl Public School building has a large selection from many dealers. Located 3.25 miles east on U.S. 63, 635-3655. Open daily, May–October.

Trego Cabin Shop features Northwoods-themed artwork, crafts, and furniture, much of it locally made. Located behind the Dinner Bell Restaurant, 635-9690. Open Wednesday–Sunday.

Windmill Crafts & Gifts has an inventory similar to the Trego Cabin Shop's plus some Wisconsin food items. Located behind the Dinner Bell Restaurant, 635-9571. Open daily April through December.

Outdoor Rentals

Jack's Canoe and Tube Rental, two blocks east on U.S. 63, 635-3300, rents canoes, kayaks, tubes, and splashboats and has a shuttle service.

Log Cabin Resort and Campground, at the junction of U.S. 53/63, 635-2959, rents canoes, kayaks, tubes, splashboats, and fishing boats and has a shuttle service.

Namekagon Outfitters, 0.5 mile west on Hwy E, 0.25 mile north on Pair O' Lakes Road, 635-2015, 800/547-9028, rents canoes and tubes and has a shuttle service.

Quiet Sports Outfitters, at the junction of U.S. 53/63, 635-9700, rents (and sells) canoes, kayaks, and camping gear and has a shuttle service. They also guide sea kayak trips to the Apostle Islands.

Where to Eat

Join the crowd at the **Trego Dinner Bell Restaurant**, at U.S. 53/63 and Hwy E, 635-3271, for basic family fare of sandwiches, salads, steaks, seafood, and daily specials, including a Friday night buffet. Breakfast is served all day. Open daily for breakfast, lunch, and dinner.

Where to Stay

Bed-and-Breakfast

The Stout Trout, W4244 Hwy F, 466-2790, is 10 miles northeast of town in a restored 1920s fishing lodge on a private bay on Gull Lake. The four guest rooms have private attached baths. You can borrow a boat or bike, wander around the 40-acre property, relax on the large deck, or swing in a hammock. Guests enjoy a full breakfast.

Other Lodging

Trego Inn Motel, half a mile south on U.S. 53/63, 635-3204, 800/681-5939, has 12 rooms.

Trego Park Campground, half a mile north on U.S. 53, 635-6075, has 45 RV sites with full hookups and three tent sites. The campground is located on the Namekagon River by the Old Iron Bridge and has showers, game area, playground, boat launch, and dump station. Open May through October. Reservations accepted.

Emergencies

Call 911. The nearest hospital is in Spooner.

More Information

Trego Chamber of Commerce, P.O. Box 5, Trego 54888, 800/367-3306.

Birchwood

As the giant fiberglass bluegill that greets you says, this is the Bluegill Capital of Wisconsin. The massive fish is the only bit of tackiness you'll find here, however, as this quaint village of 456 radiates old-fashioned, small town charm and is becoming increasingly popular as a vacation destination.

The village, named for the abundant white birch found in the area, was founded in 1901 during the logging era, and logging still plays a role with the Birchwood Lumber and Veneer Company being an important industry.

Things to See and Do

The **Birchwood Area Museum** has a small display of historic artifacts housed in an old log cabin. Of particular interest are a mounted albino deer and a logging camp diorama. Outside is a fully loaded logging sled and large steam engine from 1895. Located at Main Street and Elm Avenue. Open 11–3 Friday and Saturday, Memorial Day weekend to Labor Day.

The **Howard A. Morey Homestead** is being restored inside and out to reflect a typical family home from the early 1900s when it was built. Located on Park Avenue, one block west of Main Street. Currently it is open only during special events, but at other times someone at the museum might take you over for a look.

Birchwood Riding Stables offer horseback trail rides on their facility or extended trips to the nearby Blue Hills. Pony rides are available for the little ones. Located two miles east on Hwy 48 then three miles south on Hwy F, 354-7342. Open Tuesday–Sunday, Memorial Day weekend to Labor Day, and weekends by appointment the rest of the year. $

One of the best, and least known, canoeing areas in the state lies north of Birchwood in the Washburn County Forest. **The Sawmill Lake and Loyhead Lake Primitive Canoe Routes** connect 16 small, undeveloped lakes within a 5,000-acre designated Primitive Management Area. Maps of both routes, showing the short, marked portages, are available at the adjacent 21-site Sawmill Lake Campground. Also at the campground are a picnic area, dock, and short hiking trail. Sawmill Lake is located one mile north on Hwy D, six miles north on Hwy T, and two miles north on Birchwood Fire Lane. Loyhead Lake is another 0.75 mile north. For more information call 635-2886.

Events

Celebrate Wisconsin's official state dance at the **Birchwood Polka Celebration Festival** held the last weekend in June. Dance to the sounds of a dozen top bands from around the U.S. on two huge dance floors and experience a polka mass on Sunday.

The **Birchwood Bluegill Festival**, held the third weekend in July, features a parade, firemen's water fight, horse pull, logging demonstrations, wagon rides, sporting events, talent show, street dance, live music, and the (coveted?) coronation of the Bluegill Queen. Of course, it wouldn't be complete without a prize for the person who catches the biggest bluegill.

Shopping

Just Rite on Main is a large store filled with crafts, collectibles, porcelain dolls, and antiques. Most new items in the store are wholesale priced. Located at the corner of Main Street and Hwy 48, 354-3279. Open daily, May through December, and most days January through April.

The Porch has an interesting collection of clothing, gifts, crafts, and gourmet food items. Located at the corner of Main Street and Park Avenue, 354-7087. Open daily, April through December.

At **The Santa Cellar**, Vickie Vaughn's designer porcelain Santas show Kris Kringle as you've never seen him before. There are also non-Christmas-related crafts, paintings, and prints. Located at 213 Main St., 354-3672. Open daily May through December.

Golf

The 18-hole **Tagalong Golf Course**, one of the first in the state, was modeled after St. Andrew's, going so far as to import the seed for the greens and the construction supervisors from Scotland. Located one mile southwest on Hwy 48 then two miles south on Loch Lomand Boulevard, 354-3458, 800/657-4843.

Bicycling

The **Tuscobia State Trail** follows a former railroad bed for 74 miles between Rice Lake and Park Falls. The trail is popular with ATV riders and is also suitable for mountain bikes, but it has not been surfaced for road bikes. For more information contact the DNR at 634-6513.

Outdoor Rentals

Seasonal Power Toys, half a mile east of Main Street on Hwy 48, 354-3886, rents snowmobiles and ATVs.

Where to Eat

The **Birch Lake Inn**, at Hwy D and Main Street, 354-3182, is a popular restaurant and lounge overlooking the lake. The menu ranges from basic sandwiches, salads, seafood, steaks, and pizza to fancier options, such as chicken saltimbocca and penne à la caprise. Nightly specials include prime rib and all-you-can-eat buffets. Enjoy outdoor seating during summer evenings. Open daily for dinner.

The Birchwood Cafe, at Main Street and Birch Avenue, 354-3000, has basic diner fare of sandwiches, salads, daily specials, and breakfast served all day. Open daily for breakfast and lunch.

The Porch, at Main Street and Park Avenue, 354-7087, is a relaxing, slightly upscale coffee shop and deli that serves sandwiches, salads, fresh bakery, and pizza as well as snacks like homemade fudge and ice cream. It doesn't get any more relaxing than the large wrap-around porch with an outdoor grill where you can char-broil bison brats and burgers. Enjoy live folk music on Thursday nights. Open daily for breakfast, lunch, and dinner, April through December.

Where to Stay

Bed-and-Breakfasts

The Cobblestone, 319 Main St., 354-3494, 800/659-4883, is a simple but elegant turn-of-the-century home on the edge of town. The five antique-filled guest rooms share two baths. A full breakfast is served in the formal dining room or outdoors on the relaxing porch.

The Farm, 718 Main St., 354-3367, is a classic 1904 farmhouse on a still working farm just south of town. The five guest rooms share three baths. Stables are available if you'd like to bring your own horse and ride around the 200 acres of fields and forests. A continental breakfast is served in the morning.

Other Lodging

Birchwood Motel, 601 E. Hwy 48, 354-7706, has 8 rooms with cable TV.

Dalen's Resort, 1.5 miles east on Hwy 48 then two miles north on Hwy F on Big Chetac Lake, 354-3570, 888/354-3570, has 10 two-bedroom cottages with kitchens, cable TV, and screened porches with swings. A boat is provided with each rental; guests may use the paddle boats and canoes or rent a pontoon. On dry land are a playground and horseshoe pits. Weekly rentals only during the summer.

The village-owned **Doolittle Park and Campground**, half a mile north on Hwy D then half a mile east on Hinman Drive, has 40 campsites on Big Birch Lake with electric and cable TV hookups plus showers and a dump station. There is also a beach, playground, picnic area, and boat launch.

There's no place like **Stout's Lodge—Island of Happy Days**, 354-3646, 800/690-2650. The Adirondack-style lodge, listed on the National Register of Historic Places, sits on a peaceful 26-acre island in Red Cedar Lake. In 1903 Frank Stout, one of the country's wealthiest men, used $1.5 million of his inherited family fortune to build the retreat of his dreams: an elaborate 31-room log summer home with no detail overlooked. Today guests can indulge themselves in the 33 guest rooms in the main lodge and other estate buildings. Most rooms are furnished with antiques and have fireplaces, plus some have screened porches and kitchens. Resort amenities include volleyball, clay tennis courts, hiking trails, swimming area, boats and canoes for guest use, exercise room, and even a spa where you can get a massage, facial, or body wrap. A continental breakfast is included, and lunch and dinner are available at the highly regarded restaurant. Regular boat service is provided to the mainland. Open May through October.

Camping is available at **Sawmill Lake** (see p . 132).

Emergencies

Call 911. Lakeview Medical Center, 1100 N. Main St., Rice Lake, 234-1515.

More Information

Birchwood Area Lakes Association, P.O. Box 9, Birchwood 54817, 354-7846, 800/236-2252.

Chapter 9
St. Croix Valley
Grantsburg, Siren, Webster, Danbury

Some 10,000 years ago, as the last glacier to blanket Wisconsin retreated, an ice dam blocked the St. Croix River forming Glacial Lake Grantsburg, which covered most of what is now Burnett County. As it slowly drained it left behind over 500 smaller lakes and the region's sandy soil. The prolific lakes and river have prompted locals to call this area the Fishbowl of Wisconsin. Anglers aren't the only ones who appreciate Burnett County's natural bounty; it offers some fantastic territory for almost any outdoor pursuit, from biking to canoeing to hiking to wildlife viewing.

Grantsburg, as the gateway to most of the area's natural wonders, is the main destination here, but the small towns that grew up on the once busy rail line running between the Twin Cities and the Twin Ports are worth a stop. The trains are gone, but passengers still roll through along the line that has been converted into the Gandy Dancer Trail (p. 147). You may not have heard of any of these off-the-beaten-path villages, but if you've had your fill of nature you can soak up some small town charm.

Grantsburg

With 1,231 people Grantsburg is the largest community in Burnett County. The village was named for Ulysses S. Grant, a popular figure (at least in the North) at the time the village was founded in 1865. If you have any doubts about the abundance of wildlife in the surrounding wilderness, consider that bear encounters in town are anything but rare.

Things to See and Do

The **Grantsburg Area Historical Museum**, housed in an 1883 Methodist church, hosts changing historical exhibits about the area. Behind the church is the old Burnett County Jail (1870–1902). You can take a peek inside even when the museum is not open. Located at 133 W. Wisconsin Ave., 463-2573. Open 1–4 Sundays from Memorial Day weekend to Labor Day. Wheelchair accessible.

A unique sight is the life-size wood sculpture of hometown hero Anders Gustav Anderson, better known as **Big Gust**, who stood 7 feet 6 inches and weighed 360 pounds. You can listen to a tape recording of his story and compare shoe sizes. Located in front of the villages offices at 416 S. Pine St.

Surrounding the small lake of the same name is 35-acre **Memory Lake Park**. Enjoy a picnic area, playground, and hiking trail and watch a resident flock of Canada geese. The 12 km **Grantsburg Nordic Ski Trail** starts in the park. Located on the west side of town at Oak Street and Olson Drive.

The mix of wetlands, lakes, forest, and barrens makes the 27,467-acre **Crex Meadows Wildlife Area** one of the best wildlife-viewing spots in the state. Many threatened and endangered species have prospered here, including greater prairie chicken, trumpeter swan, bald eagle, osprey, peregrine falcon, and timber wolf. You might also spot a bear, badger, otter, beaver, common loon, golden eagle, or sharp-tailed grouse. You can watch the latter perform its fascinating mating dance from mid-April to mid-May from a reservable viewing blind. Each fall thousands of geese, ducks, and sandhill cranes stop here during their migration. Most visitors follow the 24-mile self-guided auto tour. There are also hiking trails, cross-country ski trails, and a picnic area where free camping is allowed from September through December. The refuge office, one mile north on Hwy F, 463-2896, houses a small nature center. Plans are underway for a much larger facility in the next few years.

The 13,197-acre **Fish Lake Wildlife Area**, three miles south of Grantsburg, has no designated auto tour or hiking trails, but it is still worth a visit. Like Crex, there is abundant wildlife to observe and miles of service roads to drive or hike. You can pick up maps at the Crex office or the hilltop overlook of Grettum Flowage along Hwy 48. In the center of the property, on Stolte Road, at the north end of the Dueholm Flowage, is another overlook.

The 19,602-acre **Governor Knowles State Forest** is a narrow thread of forest, wetlands, barrens, and sandstone cliffs stretching for 55 miles along the beautiful St. Croix River. Besides outstanding canoeing (see St. Croix National Scenic Riverway, p. 136) there are 41.5 miles of hiking trails, 35 miles of equestrian trails (connected to Grantsburg by another 18-mile trail), and 8.5 miles of cross-country ski trails. There is no developed campground, but there is a horse rider camping area with no facilities, backpacking is allowed with a permit, and St. Croix Riverway campsites are found along the river. All are free. A 31-site campground, along the St. Croix River at Hwy 70, should be open in 1999. The forest headquarters is on Hwy 70 at the southwest edge of town, 463-2898. Here you will find some historical displays and a short nature trail. $ for horse and ski trails.

You can get the lowdown on the **St. Croix National Scenic Riverway** (p. 136) at the **Marshland Visitor Center**. Educational displays are aimed primarily at children but of interest to all. Located four miles west on Hwy 70, on the Minnesota side of the river, 320/629-2148. Open 8:30–5 daily, Memorial Day weekend to Labor Day, and weekends in May and September. Wheelchair accessible.

The riverway's **Sandrock Cliff Trail** is in the Governor Knowles State Forest. The beautiful five-mile trail along the St. Croix River can be accessed just north of the Hwy 70 wayside. It is a great hike and is groomed for cross-country skiing.

Take a guided horseback ride on 130 wooded acres at **Lakeside Trails**. They also have pony rides for small children and hay rides. Located six miles east on Hwy 70 then five miles south on Little Wood Lake Road (which becomes Spirit Lake Road), 327-8572. Open Wednesday–Sunday weather permitting. $

Scenic Drive

Besides the auto tour through Crex Meadows described above, you can pick up a map of a 40-mile auto tour of the Governor Knowles State Forest at the forest headquarters. Scog Road just southwest of Grantsburg is a designated **Wisconsin Rustic Road.**

Events

Among the many events at **Big Gust Days**, held the first weekend in June, are a soap box derby, antique car and tractor show, kiddie parade, queen pageant, live music, and giant garage sale.

The county's biggest event, bringing in over 25,000 spectators, is the **World Championship Snowmobile Watercross**, held the third weekend in July, which has oval and drag races *on* Memory Lake. This is the nation's third largest snowmobiling event in any season. The sport of watercross, which began right here, is something you really have to see to believe. Other activities during the weekend include a vintage snowmobile show, live music, and fireworks. $

Shopping

People go out of their way to stop at the **Cheese Store** for world champion Fancy brand cheeses. They sell over 50 varieties of cheese plus ice cream, soft yogurt, and a full spread of grocery items. Located at the Burnett Dairy Cooperative, five miles east on Hwy 70, 689-2748. Open daily.

The Willows sells antiques, crafts, dried florals, and custom rustic furniture. Located at 110 Main St., 463-2746. Open Tuesday–Saturday.

Golf

The 9-hole **Grantsburg Municipal Golf Course** is right in town at 333 W. St. George Ave., 463-2300.

Outdoor Rentals

Wild River Outfitters, a half mile east of the St. Croix River on Hwy 70, 463-2254, has canoe and kayak rentals and a shuttle service.

Where to Eat

Gin Rickey's Restaurant & Lounge, just west of town on Hwy 70, 463-2967, has a small menu with a large variety; choose from Mexican, sandwiches, steaks, chicken, and seafood. Open daily for lunch and dinner.

Kozy Kitchen, 827 S. Pine St., 463-2200, has basic family-style meals including sandwiches, salads, broasted chicken and daily specials, such as all-you-can-eat BBQ ribs and a Friday fish fry. Eat in the smoke-free dining room or choose the outdoor walkup service. Open daily for breakfast, lunch, and dinner.

Where to Stay

The municipally owned **James N. McNally Campground**, adjoining Memory Lake Park, has 38 sites (21 electric and 14 with water, wheelchair-accessible sites), showers, and dump station. Open April to early November, weather permitting.

Wood River Inn Motel, just west of town on Hwy 70, 463-2541, has 30 rooms, including some whirlpool suites, with cable TV.

Camping is available at the **Governor Knowles State Forest** and **Crex Meadows Wildlife Area**, both described above.

Emergencies

Call 911. Burnett Medical Center, 257 W. St. George Ave., 463-5353.

More Information

Village of Grantsburg, 416 S. Pine St., Grantsburg 54840, 463-2405.

Siren

Other than the Gandy Dancer Trail, there is little to do in this village of 867 besides eat, sleep, and shop, but because it is at the crossroads of Hwys 35 and 70 it is a popular stop with far more hotels, restaurants, and shops than any other town in Burnett County.

The town was settled by Swedish pioneers. The town's first postmaster named it Syren, the Swedish word for lilac, a flower he adored. Postal headquarters changed it to Siren, assuming the word was misspelled.

Gandy Dancer Trail

This 98-mile interstate rail-to-trail connecting Superior with St. Croix Falls, Wisconsin, has two distinct sections. The 47 miles of trail south of Hwy 77 (at the town of Danbury) is surfaced with crushed limestone and is ideal for bike riders. From December through April snowmobiles and ATVs can use this section if the snow base is four inches or more. The 51 miles north of Hwy 77, which has not been surfaced, is a wilder ride with fewer communities and roads along the route. It can be used by hikers, mountain bikers, horseback riders, ATV riders, and snowmobilers.

The trail is named in honor of the "Gandy Dancer Crews" who maintained the rail line by hand in the early 1900s. The men, using tools from the Gandy Manufacturing Company, swung their tools and moved their feet in unison by following song-like calls.

A daily or seasonal state trail pass is required of all bicyclists over 16 years of age on the southern section of the trail. Passes are available in many places in all communities along the trail. Call 800/788-3164 for additional trail information.

Things to See and Do

Northwest of town, the 6,138-acre **Amsterdam Sloughs Wildlife Area** is mostly wooded with several large flowages. It is a great place to hike and observe wildlife. Not to be missed is the 500-acre Black Brook Flowage along Hwy D, which is home to a large great blue heron rookery as well as nesting bald eagle and osprey. Maps are available at the Crex Meadows Wildlife Area office (p. 144).

The village's summer fun spot is **Crooked Lake Park**, which has a beach, boat launch, wheelchair-accessible fishing pier, playground, volleyball, and picnic area. Located at the north end of town on Hwy 35/70.

From the outside the **Little Turtle Hertel Express** appears to be just another gas station/convenience store, but what draws people here is the small and surprisingly quiet casino with slots, video poker and keno, and pull-tabs. You must be 21 years old to enter. Located 10 miles east of Siren on Hwy 70, 349-5658. Open daily. Wheelchair accessible.

Right next door in the St. Croix Tribal Center is **Sand Lake Bingo**, 800/236-2195. A lunch counter and smoke shop are open during bingo sessions. Games are held on Monday, Wednesday, Friday, and Saturday nights and Sunday afternoons. Wheelchair accessible.

Events

The entire village kicks back during **Siren Summerfest Days**, held in late July or early August. Events include pie-eating and watermelon-seed-spitting contests, antique tractor and small engine show, hot-air balloon rides, kiddie parade, talent show, sidewalk sales, arts and crafts, street dance, live music, and a beauty pageant.

Shopping

Siren is an antique lovers town with most stores, unless otherwise noted, at the northern junction of Hwys 35 and 70, 1.5 miles north of town.

Antiques on the River, 349-7177, also sells some crafts, including a year-round Christmas selection. Open Friday–Sunday in April and daily except Tuesday from May through September.

Back Door Antiques has a good selection. Located downtown at 7740 W. Main St., 349-7151. Open daily.

Country Barn Gifts & Antiques, 349-2878, has a large selection of arts and crafts and also a year-round Christmas selection. Open daily.

Crossroad Antiques Mall, 349-2818, with 20 dealers has by far the largest selection of antiques. Don't miss the separate building for furniture out back. Open daily, April through October.

It's amazing how much **Timberland Gifts & Goods** packs into its small log cabin shop, not to mention the variety. Choose between gourmet foods, homemade fudge, dolls, moccasins, bird feeders and houses, giant barrel saunas, rustic furniture, and lots of crafts. Located at the north end of town on Hwy 35/70, 349-5525. Open daily.

Bicycling

The **Gandy Dancer Trail** (p. 147) passes through town.

Outdoor Rentals

Shoreline Sports, two miles north on Hwy 35, 349-2246, rents snowmobiles.

Where to Eat

Fancy Freeze Drive-In, at the north end of town on Hwy 35, 349-5209, has sandwiches, chicken, and lots of ice cream. Either eat outside or enjoy the old-fashioned car hop service. Open daily for lunch and dinner, April to October.

Sister's on the Shore, 6699 Hwy 70, 349-2445, has fine dining and cocktails overlooking the Clam Lake Narrows 3.5 miles northeast of town. The main dining options are steaks, seafood, and sandwiches, plus many nightly specials, such as a Thursday seafood buffet, Friday fish fry, Saturday prime rib. Open daily except Tuesday for dinner and also Thursday–Sunday for lunch with a Sunday breakfast buffet.

Sunshine Family Restaurant, 1.5 miles north at the junction of Hwys 35 and 70, 349-2570, offers sandwiches, salads, chicken, and steaks and serves breakfast all day. They are rightfully proud of their homemade pies. An ice cream shop is located out front. Open daily for breakfast, lunch, and dinner.

Where to Stay

Bed-and-Breakfasts

Forgotten Tymes Country Inn, 7420 Tower Rd., 349-5837, 800/SIRENWI, is a quiet country estate with four restored log cabins. Some of the large units have full kitchens, Jacuzzis, decks, and fireplaces. The large estate has horses and offers canoeing on the lake or hiking and cross-country skiing on the trail through the wooded grounds. A continental breakfast is served in the main lodge.

Lilac Village, 7665 Bradley St., 349-7012, harks back to a simpler era in a beautiful 1936 Dutch Colonial home. The three guest rooms have private baths, two attached, and one has a whirlpool tub. Guests can relax out back on the porch or the sunroom and are served a full breakfast in the morning.

Other Lodging

Best Western Northwoods Lodge, at the southern junction of Hwys 35 and 70, 349-7800, has 40 rooms, including some whirlpool suites, in a modern log building with cable TV, indoor pool, whirlpool, sauna, and free continental breakfast.

The Lodge at Crooked Lake, 24271 Hwy 35, 349-2500, 877/843-5634, a newly built classic Northwoods log lodge, has 70 rooms, including some deluxe whirlpool suites with fireplaces, with cable TV, indoor pool, whirlpool, sauna, game room, exercise room, and free continental breakfast.

Pine Wood Motel, 23862 Hwy 35, 349-5225, has 14 rooms with cable TV.

Emergencies

Call 911. The nearest hospital is in Grantsburg.

More Information

Siren Area Chamber of Commerce, P.O. Box 57, Siren 54872, 349-2273, 800/788-3164. A Burnett County Tourist Information Center is located in the lobby of the Best Western Northwoods Lodge.

Webster

This village of 628 people situated between the Yellow and Clam Rivers was named for American statesman Daniel Webster. The local legend is that an early citizen named Ed Peet once said, "If Webster is good enough to name a dictionary it's good enough to name this town."

Things to See and Do

At **Folle Avoine Historical Park** the Burnett County Historical Society and the St. Croix Ojibwe have meticulously reconstructed the fur trading posts of the competing XY and North West Companies and an Ojibwe village along the Yellow River. Interpretive guides in period dress transport visitors back to 1802, allowing them to experience the life and culture of the early pioneers and Native Americans. The site is listed on the National Register of Historic Places. The visitor center houses a fur trade museum, theater, gift shop, and the Wild Rice Cafe, which serves Native American and fur trade era foods. The cafe is open for Sunday brunch and special events. The park is on Hwy U, 2.75 miles west of Hwy 35, 866-8890. Open 9–5 Wednesday–Sunday from Memorial Day weekend to Labor Day, with tours departing on the hour. Special events are held throughout the year. A five-mile cross-country ski trail is open on winter weekends. Wheelchair accessible. $

The St. Croix River is the main draw for paddlers in these parts, but there are other scenic and leisurely **canoeing** options nearby. A half mile north of town is the **Yellow River** with a small canoe landing along Hwy 35. The nearest put-in for the **Clam River** is at Meenon County Park, about 1.5 miles south on Hwy 35. Both rivers eventually empty into the larger St. Croix (p. 136).

Events

The **Great Folle Avoine Fur Trade Rendezvous**, held the third weekend in July at Folle Avoine Historical Park (p. 150), takes its regular production to another level. People come from all over to participate in the lifestyle of old. There are cooking, craft, blacksmith, and outdoor skill demonstrations; wilderness skill competitions like black powder shooting and knife throwing; and traders' row where you can buy or barter for period goods, such as clothing, candles, cookware, jewelry. $ for park admission.

Shopping

Lake Country Mall, with over 200 dealers, has a truly huge selection of crafts, including one room stocked year-round with Christmas items. There are also antiques from another dozen dealers. Located on Hwy 35 on the north side of town, 866-7670. Open daily, May through October, and Monday–Saturday (Sundays by chance) from January to April.

Ma & Pa's General Store has a large selection of antiques, much of it sold on consignment. Located at 7444 W. Main St., 866-4860. Open Tuesday–Saturday from June through October.

Golf

There are three golf courses to choose from near Webster: **Fox Run Golf Course**, two miles north on Hwy 35, 866-7953, has 9 holes plus another 9-hole par 3 course; **Voyager Village Country Club**, one mile north on Hwy 35, 14 miles east on Hwy A, and three miles north on Kilkare Road, 259-3911, has 18 challenging holes plus a separate 9-hole par 3 course; the 9-hole **Yellow Lake Golf Course**, 3.5 miles north on Hwy 35 then 0.75 mile west on Hwy U, 866-7107, is one of the state's most unique courses. It has no rough and some of the last sand greens, plus special balls for night and winter golf. There are also 9 holes of mini-golf.

Bicycling

The **Gandy Dancer Trail** (p. 147) passes through town.

Outdoor Rentals

Hayes Pro Bike & Ski, 7461 W. Main St., 866-8101, sits just off the Gandy Dancer Trail and rents bikes and cross-country skis.

Where to Eat

North View Drive Inn, at the north end of town on Hwy 35, 866-7642, serves sandwiches, chicken, and ice cream, all with old-fashioned car hop service. Open daily for lunch and dinner from May through September.

Enjoy pizza and other Italian dishes at **Zia Louisa**, just north of town on Hwy 35, 866-4260. Even many American dishes such as steaks, hamburgers, and hot dogs have been Italianized. Open for dinner Wednesday–Monday, May through September, and Thursday–Monday, October through April.

Where to Stay

Webster Motel, Hwy 35 at Main Street, 866-8951, has 14 basic rooms with cable TV.

Emergencies

Call 911. The nearest hospital is in Grantsburg.

More Information

Webster Area Chamber of Commerce, P.O. Box 48, Webster 54893, 866-4251.

ST. CROIX VALLEY 153

Danbury

Just 200 people call Danbury home, but it is still a bustling community, thanks to the popular casino. In the early nineteenth century the Ojibwe established a village at this strategic spot where the Yellow River empties into the St. Croix River. A sawmill brought the first White settlers to the area. Blueberries were especially abundant, and when the railroad came to town it shipped so many of them to other cities that it was known as the Blueberry Special.

Things to See and Do

The **Hole in the Wall Casino**, operated by the St. Croix Ojibwe, offers blackjack, slots, video poker and keno, and pull-tabs. There is also a smoke shop, saloon, restaurant, and live entertainment. You must be 21 or older to enter. Located in town at the junction of Hwys 35 and 77, 656-3444, 800/BET-U-WIN. Open daily. Wheelchair accessible.

The highlight of the entire 98-mile Gandy Dancer Trail (p. 147) is the **520-foot bridge** spanning the St. Croix River. It is located just half a mile north of town.

There are several landings for the **St. Croix National Scenic Riverway** (p. 136) nearby.

Black Bear's Den, a combination gas station–liquor store–gift and snack shop, displays a **former world record bear** (see pg. 70) that weighed in at 635 pounds and measured 7 feet 3/4 inches. Located in town on Hwy 77, just west of Hwy 35. Open 8–10 daily.

The people of Danbury escape the summer heat at **Ralph Larrabee Park**, which has a small beach and picnic area on Round Lake. It is adjacent to the Gandy Dancer Trail (p. 147). Located just west of Hwy 35 on Round Lake Road, one mile south of town.

You can give **dog sledding** a try at Paw Tuck Away Kennels. Either enjoy a brief introduction with the dogs or arrange an extended mushing trip. Get a hint of things to come during summer clinics beginning in August. Call 656-4419 to make a reservation or get more information. **$**

Although it's far off the beaten path, the 5,000-acre **Namekagon Barrens Wildlife Area** is worth a visit. The variety of grassland species attracts many birdwatchers to the barrens, but the rare shrub prairie habitat is uniquely beautiful in its own right, especially in the summer months when the prairie flowers bloom. Each spring, peaking from mid-April to mid-May, sharp-tailed grouse perform their fascinating mating dance at dawn. Call the DNR at 635-4092 to reserve a viewing blind. To get there, take Hwy 35 ten miles north to St. Croix Trail and go east for eight miles to Dry Landing Road which, along with several others, leads through the area. There is a smaller section a few miles south along the Namekagon River. It is visible from Namekagon Trail and Springbrook Trail Roads.

The St. Croix Ojibwe

When the U.S. Government and the Ojibwe signed the Treaty of La Pointe in 1855, which established reservations in Wisconsin, all the chiefs of the various Ojibwe bands, except Chief Yabanse of the St. Croix Ojibwe, came to represent their interests. Chief Yabanse did not make the trip since he believed the government had already promised his people that they could remain on their lands. Because no one spoke for their interests the St. Croix band was not recognized by the government and thus received no land. They became known as the "Lost Tribe of the Ojibwe."

After more than eight decades without a home the St. Croix Reservation was officially founded in 1938 by the secretary of the interior. The reservation is made up of a noncontiguous parcel of land scattered over 11 communities. About half of the land and tribal members are in Burnett County as is the tribal headquarters located in the community of Big Sand, 10 miles east of Siren. The rest of the reservation is in Barron, Polk, and Douglas Counties in Wisconsin and Pine County in east central Minnesota. Though the tracts are small, they center on historic village sites of the St. Croix Ojibwe's homeland.

Events

The **Wild Rice Powwow**, held in August at the Hole in the Wall Casino, is hosted by the St. Croix Ojibwe. Dancers, drummers, and singers from across the Midwest and Canada perform and compete. You can also sample native foods and crafts. $

Shopping

Earthbound Studio has many high-quality craft items, most with a nature theme, plus candles and gourmet foods. Located at the south edge of town on Hwy 35, 656-3854. Open Tuesday–Sunday, May through August, and Saturday-Sunday, September through December.

Besides doing custom embroidery and screen printing **Homestead Embroidery** has a small selection of antiques and crafts. Located at 7523 Main St., 656-3220. Open Monday–Saturday year-round, except closed Tuesdays from January through April.

Koester's Kaleidoscope sells specialty coffees, herbs, and spices and has a good selection of antiques and crafts. Located at 7533 Main St., 656-4595. Open Thursday–Monday.

Bicycling

The **Gandy Dancer Trail** (p. 147) passes through town.

Outdoor Rentals

Gulden's, on Hwy 35 at the south edge of town, 656-4402, has canoe and inner tube rentals plus a shuttle service.

Where to Eat

The **Inside Out Cafe**, right next to the casino, 656-3119, has sandwiches, broasted chicken, seafood, daily specials, and lower prices than the restaurant in the casino. Open daily for breakfast, lunch, and dinner.

The **Loose Change Cafe**, located in the casino, serves up sandwiches, seafood, steaks, and pasta on the regular menu, plus a variety of daily specials such as chow mein and prime rib. Open daily for breakfast, lunch, and dinner.

Where to Stay

The **Hole in the Wall Hotel & RV Park**, 656-4333, 800/BET-U-WIN, is adjacent to the casino. The hotel has 38 rooms, whirlpool, game room, and free continental breakfast. The RV park has 35 electric sites and showers. Those gambling at the casino are eligible for discounts.

Emergencies

Call 911. The nearest hospital is in Grantsburg.

More Information

Danbury Chamber of Commerce, P.O. Box 196, Danbury 54830, 656-3292.

Index

A.B.C. Raceway 62
Aerial Lift Bridge 76, 77, 86
Alvord Theater 59
Amnicon Falls State Park 80, 85
Amsterdam Sloughs Wildlife Area 148
Anna-Gene County Park 97
Apostle Highlands Ski Trails 5
Apostle Islands Cruise Service 3, 9
Apostle Islands National Lakeshore 2-3, 13, 21, 33
Ashland ix, x, 8, 55-65, 79
Ashland Agricultural Research Station 58
Ashland Breakwater Lighthouse 57
Ashland Historical Society Museum 56
Ashland Main Street Historic District 56

Bad River Bingo 66
Bad River Casino 66, 67
Bad River Falls 66
Bad River Fish Hatchery 66
Bad River Reservation 13-14, 20, 65-67
BAMBA mountain-bike trail system 26, 28
Bark Bay Slough State Natural Area 35
Barker's Island 75-76, 81, 82
Bass Lake Interpretive Trail 47
Bayfield ix, 1-13, 14, 20, 24
Bayfield County Courthouse 25
Bayfield Heritage Association Museum 3
Bayfield Public Library 5
Bayfield State Fish Hatchery 4
Bayfront Festival Park 88
Bayside Sounds 81
Bayview Park 57, 58
Bayview Town Park 26
Bear Country Sporting Goods 47
Beautiful Pine Walk 71
Beaver Brook Trail 128
Berry farms 8
Bibon Swamp State Natural Area 47
Big Bay State Park 16, 20
Big Bay Town Park 16, 20
Big Gust 144
Big Rock County Park 26, 29
Big Top Chautauqua 8
Biggest and last sleigh-hauled log 71
Birch Grove Trail 26
Birchbark canoe trip 106-107
Birchwood 138-142
Birchwood Area Museum 138-139
Birkebeiner Trail 41, 109
Black Bear's Den 153
Black Lake Trail 108

Boat Watcher's Hotline 77
Booth Cooperage Museum 3-4
Brighton Beach 92
Broad Street Beach 5-6
Brule 101-104
Brule River Classics 102, 103
Brule River State Fish Hatchery 102
Brule River State Forest 97, 98, 102, 103
Brule-St. Croix Historic Portage Trail 97
Bulik's Amusement Center 128
Burlington Northern Ore Docks 78

Cable 40-46, 136
Cable Natural History Museum 40-41
CAMBA trail system 42, 43, 47, 52, 112
Canal Park 85-86, 89, 93, 95
Capser and Nucy Meech hiking trails 16
Capt'n J's Miniature Golf 75
Chamber music concerts 8
Chapple Avenue area 57
Chester Bowl 93
Chequamegon National Forest 16, 27, 28, 29, 41, 42, 46, 47, 48-49, 50, 53, 54, 68-69, 70, 71-72, 73, 98, 108-109, 110, 118, 136
Chequamegon Theatre Association 59-62
Chippewa Flowage 72, 109, 110, 116, 118
Chippewa Queen Tours 109
Christ Church 5, 8
Clam Lake 72
Clam River 151
Clover Town Park 35, 36
College Street Park Ski Trail 128
Col. D.D. Gaillard 76
Congdon Park Trail 94-95
Connors Point 77
Copper Falls State Park 68, 69, 70, 98
Cornucopia 31-35
Crex Meadows Wildlife Area 144, 145, 146, 148
Crooked Lake Park 148

Danbury 147, 153-155
Davidson Windmill 78
Day Lake Recreation Area 48, 71
Dead Horse Run Trail 71
The Depot 89-90, 94, 95
Dog sledding
  George Tresnak 69
  Lazy Susan's B&B 33
  Madeline Island Dog Sled Trips 16
  Paw Tuck Away Kennels 153
Douglas County Ski Trail 98

INDEX

Douglas County Wildlife Area 97
Drummond 46-47, 50
Drummond Historical Museum 46
Drummond Trail 47
Drummond Woods Interpretive Trail 47
Duluth x, 74-75, 76, 77, 85-95
Duluth Curling Club 88
Duluth Entertainment Convention Center (DECC) 88
Duluth, Missabe, and Iron Range Railway Company observation platform 77
Duluth-Superior Dukes 92
Dwight's Point and Pokegama Wetlands State Natural Area 79

East End Park 6
East Fork Chippewa River 72
Elk 72
Enger Park 93

Fairlawn Mansion and Museum 76
Fall color tours
  Cable 41
  Hayward 110
Fiddler's Creek 107
Fish Creek Sloughs 57
Fish Lake Wildlife Area 144
Fishing charters
  Anglers All 62
  Day-O Charters 38
  Duluth's charter fishing docks 86
  Fish Lipps 34
  Gitcheegummee Guide Servide 28
  Lou's Charter Service 62
  Northern Lite Charters 38
  Nourse's Sport Fishing 9
  South Shore Charters 38
  Spoon Feeder Charters 38
  Superior Charter Dock 82
Fitger's Brewery Complex 89
Fitger's Museum and Copper Kettle Room 89
Flambeau River State Forest 109-110, 118
Folle Avoine Historical Park 150-151
Fond-Du-Luth Casino 90
Forest Lodge Library 41
Forest Lodge Nature Trail 41

Gandy Dancer Trail 143, 147, 149, 152, 153, 155
Glensheen 91
Glidden 48, 70-73, 110
Glidden Area Historical Society Museum 71
Golf
  Aken's Golf Course 112
  Apostle Highlands Golf Course 9

Ashland Elks Golf Course 62
Barker Lake Golf Course 112
Barronett Hills Golf Course 133
Botten's Green Acres 103
Butternut Hills Golf Club 133
Clam River Golf Club 133
Forest Point Golf Course 101
Forest Ridges Golf Course 43
Fox Run Golf Course 151
Grantsburg Municipal Golf Course 146
Hayward Golf & Tennis Club 112
Hidden Greens North 99
Lakeview Golf and Pizza 112
Madeline Island Golf Club 17
Mellen Country Club 69
Nemadji Municipal Golf Course 82
Norwood Golf Course 103
Pattison Park Golf Course 82
Poplar Golf Course 82
Ross' Teal Wing Golf Club 112
Roynona Creek Golf Course 112
Spider Lake Golf Resort 112
Spooner Golf Club 129
Spring Creek Golf Club 112
Tagalong Golf Course 140
Telemark Golf Course 43
Voyager Village Country Club 151
Yellow Lake Golf Course 151
Gordon 100-101, 136
Gordon Flowage Park 100, 101, 136
Gordon-Wascott Historical Museum 100
Governor Knowles State Forest 144-145, 146
Governor Tommy G. Thompson State Fish Hatchery 127
Grand Slam Adventure World 86
Grantsburg 136, 143-147
Grantsburg Area Historical Museum 143-144
Grantsburg Nordic Ski Trail 144
Great Divide National Forest Scenic Byway 72, 110
Great Divide Waside 72
Great Lakes Aquarium at Lake Superior Center 88
Grindstone Creek Casino 119
The Gym 35

Harvest States grain elevators 77
Hawk Ridge Nature Reserve 93
Hayward x, 40, 42, 48, 105-118, 135, 136
Hayward Amusement Park 107
Hayward Beach and Park 108
Hayward Mini Golf 107
Herbster 31, 35-36
The Hideout: Al Capone's Northwoods Retreat and Museum of the Roaring 20s 119, 121

Historyland   107, 113
Hokenson Brothers Fishery   21
Hole in the Wall Casino   153, 154, 155
Horseback riding
   Appa-Lolly Ranch   108
   Big Spruce Stable   69
   Birchwood Riding Stables   139
   Hay Lake Ranch   135
   Mrotek's Stables   108, 113
   Lakeside Trails   145
   The Ranch   52
Howard A. Morey Homestead   139
Hunt Hill Audubon Sanctuary   132

Ice racing
   Ashland   62
   Bayfield   9
Indianhead Arts & Education Center   133
Iron Bridge   5
Iron Bridge Nature Trail   5
Iron River   x, 24, 42, 51-54
Iron River National Fish Hatchery   51, 53
Iron River Trout Haus   51
Irvin, William A.   86, 88
Isle Vista Casino   20-21, 22

Jail (Bayfield City)   5
Joni's Beach   15
Just-4-Par Mini Golf   57

Kakagon and Bad River Sloughs   65, 66
Karpeles Manuscript Library Museum   91
Kingsbury Creek Trail   94-95
Kitchi Gammi Park   92
Kreher Park   57, 65
Kruk Art Gallery   78

La Point   13-20, 24
La Pointe Indian Cemetery   15
Lac Courte Oreilles Casino   119, 121, 122
Lac Courte Oreilles Reservation   118-122
Lake Superior and Mississippi Railroad   94
Lake Superior Maritime Visitor Center   77, 86
Lake Superior Paper Industries' paper mill tour   92
Lake Superior tug boat   87
Lake Superior Zoo   92
Lake View School   15
Lakeshore Walking Trail   25-26
Lakewalk   89
Leif Erickson Park   89
Lester Park Trail   94-95

Litle Sand Bay   3, 21, 23
Little Turtle Hertel Express   148
Lombardy Poplar   25
Long Lake Picnic Ground   26
Lost Creek Falls   32
Lucius Woods County Park   97
Lucius Woods Performing Arts Center   99
Lynch Creek   41

Madeline Island   13-20, 120
Madeline Island Bus Tours   16
Madeline Island Ferry   14
Madeline Island Historical Museum   14-15
Madeline Island Music Camp   17
Madeline Mini Golf   15
Manitou Island Fish Camp   3
Marion Park   71, 72
Marion Park Pavilion   71
Marinas
   Apostle Islands Marina   9
   Barker's Island Marina   82
   Bell Marina   33
   Buffalo Bay Marina   21
   Madeline Island Yacht Club   17
   Port of Ashland Marina & Yacht Club   62
   Port Superior Marina   9
   Port Wing Marina   38
   Roys Point Marina   22
   Siskiwit Bay Marina   33
   Washburn Marina   28
Marshall W. Alworth Planetarium   92
Maslowski Beach   57
Mellen   68-70
Mellen Area Museum   68
Mellen City   68
Memorial Park, Ashland   57-59
Memorial Park, Washburn   25, 29
Memory Lake Park   144
Meenon County Park   151
Minnesota Point   87, 88
Minnesota Slip Drawbridge   86
Moccasin Bar   107
Moon Lake Park   51-52, 54
Moquah Barrens Auto Tour   27
Morgan Falls and St. Peter's Dome   69
Mt. Ashwabay   5, 8
Mt. Valhalla Recreation Area   153-154
Mukwonago Trail   109
Museum of Woodcarving   131

Namekagon Barrens Wildlife Area   153-154
Namekagon-Court Oreilles Portage Trail   108
Namekagon Trail   41
National Fresh Water Fishing Hall of Fame and Museum   106

INDEX

North Country National Scenic Trail 47, 68, 69, 97, 98, 102
North Shore Scenic Railroad 94
Northern Great Lakes Center 56
Northwoods Beach 119, 121, 122

Odanah ix, 65
Ojibway Memorial Park 15
Old Central High School 90
Old Firehouse and Police Museum 78
Old School Memorial Park 37
OMNIMAX Theatre 87-88
Orchards and berry farms 8
Orienta Falls 37
Osaugie Trail 78, 79, 82

Park Creek Pond 97
Park Point x, 88-89
Park Point Recreation Area 88
Park Point Trail 89
Pattison State Park 80, 85
Penokee Mountain Trail 69
Penokee Overlook 69
Pigeon Lake Interpretive Trail 47
Playfront 88
Point-Detour Campground 32
Poplar 78, 82
Porcupine Lake Wilderness Area 47
Port-Town Part-Time Players 81
Port Town Trolley 93
Port Wing 31, 37-39
Powwows
    Honor the Earth Powwow 121
    Lac Courte Oreilles Schools Contest Powwow 121
    Manomin Powwow 67
    New Year's Eve Powwow 121
    Red Cliff Traditional Powwow 21
    Veterans Powwow 121
    Wild Rice Powwow 154
Prentice Park 57, 62, 65, 79

Quiet Lakes 117

Raging Rapids Waterslide 108
Railroad Memorial Museum 126, 128
Ralph Larrabee Park 153
Rainbow Lake Wilderness Area 47
Red Cliff Reservation ix, 8, 20-23
Reiten Beach 5-6
Richard I. Bong Heritage Center 78-79
Richard I. Bong Memorial 78
Rinehart Theatre 59-62
RR Hiking Trail 5, 9, 13
Rock Lake National Recreation Trail 41
Rose Garden 89
Rust-Owen Reservoir 46-47

Rustic Roads
    Lake Road 123
    Little Stone Road 123
    Scog Road 145

S.S. Meteor Whaleback Ship and Maritime Museum 76
Sailing charters
    Animaashi Sailing Co. 9
    Apostle Islands Yacht Charter Association 17
    Catchun-Sun Charters 9
    Lazy Susan's 34
    Moon Shadow Sailing 9
    Sailboats Inc. 9, 82
    Sandpiper 22
    Superior Charters 9
Sand Lake Bingo 148
Sandrock Cliff Trail 146
Sawmill Lake and Loyhead Lake Primitive Canoe Routes 139, 142
Sawyer Brook Springs Ski Trail 131
Sawyer County Historical Museum 107
Scheer's Lumberjack Shows 106
Seaman's Memorial Statue 76
Seaplane ride 89
Seven Bridges Road 93
Shack Smokehouse and Grill 81, 84
Shell Lake 130-134
Shell Lake Public Beach and Park 131
Sioux River 26
Sioux River Canoe 26, 28
Siren 147-150
Siskiwit Bay Park 32
Siskiwit Falls 32
Skyline Parkway 92-93
Solon Springs 96-100
Solon Springs Historical Museum 97
Soo Line Depot 56-57, 63
Soo Line Ore Dock 57
Spirit Mountain x, 95
Spooner x, 126-130
Springbrook Church Museum 135
Squaw Bay sea caves 26, 33
St. Croix National Scenic Riverway 41, 100, 108, 135, 136, 144, 145, 153
St. Francis Solanus Indian Mission 119, 121
St. Mary's Orthodox Church 32
Stone Lake 122-125
Stone Lake Area Historical Museum 123
Superior x, 74-85, 87, 101, 147
Superior Entry 77, 87
Superior Municipal Forest 79, 82
Superior Speedway 83
Superior Street, Duluth 90
Superior Water-Logged Lumber Company 59, 60-61

Telemark Resort   41, 42, 45-46
Tern Island   57
Third Floor Gallery   78
Thompson's West End Park   25, 29
TomKat MiniGolf   51
Tom's Burned Down Cafe
  & Phoenix Gallery   15
Top Gun Tours   28
Trego   127, 135-138
Trego Lake Trail   135
Trego Nature Trail   135
Trek and Trail   3, 9
Tri-County Corridor   52, 62, 79, 82, 102
Tuscobia State Trail   140
Tweed Museum of Art   91-92
Twin Falls Park   37

University of Minnesota/Duluth
  Aquatics Center sea kayak tours
  88-89
University of Wisconsin-Superior
  78, 80-81, 83

Vista Fleet   76, 77, 86, 95

Washburn   ix, 23-30, 48
Washburn County Historical Museum
  131
Washburn Iron Works   25
Washburn Museum and
  Cultural Center   25

Washburn Public Library   25
Washington Avenue Beach   5
Waterfront Trail   58, 62
Waverly Beach   66
Webster   150-152
West Second Street Historic District
  56
West Torch River Trail   71
Western Bayfield County Historical
  Museum   51
Western Waterfront Trail   94
White River   47
Whittlesey Creek National Wildlife
  Refuge   56
Wildlife Museum & Bar   107
Willard Munger State Trail   94
William A. Irvin   86, 88
Wilderness Walk   106
Wisconsin Great Northern Railroad
  127
Wisconsin Point   77, 78, 79, 82
Wisconsin Police and Fire Hall
  of Fame   78
World's largest black bear   70
World's largest white pine log   71

Yellow River   151

Zeeto   3